Writing the Bestseller
romantic and commercial fiction

Edited by Jane Porter
and Rebecca Lyles

TULE
PUBLISHING

What others are saying...

"Writing the Bestseller *is an apprenticeship between the covers. Where else can you find successful writers and editors guiding you through the paces of writing great fiction?!*"

—Elizabeth Boyle, New York Times Bestselling author of *Love Letters from a Duke* and *If Wishes Were Earls*

"Writing the Bestseller *will be a valuable resource for both aspiring romance writers as well as established authors who want to fine-tune their literary skills.*"

—John Charles, RWA Librarian of the Year in 2002, *Booklist* reviewer, and co-author of *Romance Today: An A-to-Z Guide to Contemporary American Romance Writers*

"*Reading* Writing the Bestseller *was like sitting down for lunch with a group of girlfriends who just so happened to be published romance and women's fiction authors. The main course is a candid examination of writing craft and publishing, and it's all served up with a hearty side of helpful hints, humor, and heart.*"

—Amy Sue Nathan, author of *The Glass Wives*, founder of womensfictionwriters.com, and freelance editor

"Chock full of some of the best advice for writers I've seen, Writing the Bestseller *may be the motivation you need to unlock that book inside you. Empowering, educating, fun, and practical all rolled into one amazing tell-all book."*

—Crystal Patriarche, founder, BookSparks and SparkPress

"Whether you're just starting your first book or just finished your fifth, Writing the Bestseller *should have a place of honor on every writer's desk. I expect that, over the years, my own copy will become dog-eared, underlined and highlighted until the pages fall out."*

—Jami Deise, author, *Keeping Score*; associate reviewer, Chick Lit Central

"This is exactly the kind of book I wish I'd had when I was starting out. And the kind of book I could honestly still use. Timeless advice from some serious masters of the craft."

—Maisey Yates, *USA Today* bestselling author of the *Silver Creek* series

*"*Writing the Bestseller *is an author's dream guide to publication. As a publicist and talk show host, I can attest that marketing a poor or under developed book can be a career ender for an author. This book teaches the author how to create their best book possible."*

—Jennifer Fusco, Owner, Market or Die Author Services, LLC. Host of Romance is On the Air, part of Authors on the Air Global Radio Network

Writing the Bestseller

© Copyright 2014 Tule Publishing Group

The Tule Publishing Group, LLC

ISBN 978-1-940296-21-0

Foreword

Welcome to the best book you'll ever find on the craft of writing romance!

When the amazing Jane Porter, who is founder and editorial director of Tule Publishing, asked me to contribute, I felt thrilled and honored. Partly because I love Tule's philosophy when it comes to authors; unlike some other publishing houses, Tule places fostering creativity, freedom and commercial success at the forefront of all it does. And also partly because I knew I would be in the company of some of the most successful romance writers in the business sharing their precious knowledge and experience. I've worked with most of them as an editor, read them all and am now joining their ranks as a writer—and, believe me, they are the greatest! They can claim audiences of millions around the world and, between them, years of crafting romance fiction in a variety of sub-genres, and also of sharing their knowledge and techniques by blogging online and lecturing at international writers' conferences.

So, this book is a unique opportunity in your journey to write great romance, a true master class. In it, you'll find a wealth of views, tips and secrets to help, stimulate and even provoke you into honing your skills and being a happy, confident writer.

Tessa Shapcott

Introduction

As a child, I loved reading so much that I couldn't stand to finish a favorite book or series and not have more to read, so in second grade I began to do my own version of fan fiction... I wrote additional books for Frank Baum's *Wizard of Oz* series, and by fourth grade, I was writing my own version of *Little Women*.

I don't even know why I had to write, I just did.

I still do.

I love the craft of writing, the story, the characters, the conflict, the motivation. But most of all, I love creating something I can give to readers, who can then get lost in the story, too.

Over the course of my career, I have met incredibly talented authors who love story and craft, too. These writers understand that readers deserve an amazing story and their commitment to craft is what helps set them apart.

Great writers understand that the reader comes first, and it's our job to push ourselves so that every story can surprise, delight, and ultimately, satisfy the reader.

The authors contributing essays and articles to this book aren't just my friends. Each and every one is a gifted, bestselling author who is passionate about the craft of writing, the publishing industry, and most of all, satisfying the reader. They've joined me in sharing their knowledge and experience so you can succeed in this business, too.

Writing the Bestseller is both practical advice, craft how-to, and an inspirational pep talk where we'll share what we've learned as bestselling authors, including the Things No One Tells You.

If something in *Writing the Bestseller* is not attributed to a specific author, I probably wrote it. The rest is (I hope) properly credited to the awesome women who have contributed to this book.

Enjoy—and best wishes for whatever your writing goals may be!

Jane Porter

Contents

PRE-WRITING

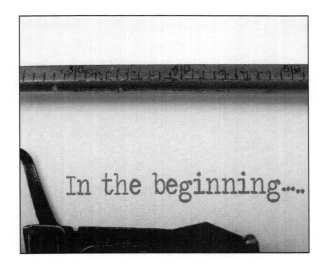

What Romance Readers Want

By Tessa Shapcott

I've worked in the women's fiction industry for over twenty-five years as an editor and a writer. Though a lot has changed in the world since the nineteen-eighties, including women's status in society, romance has proved to be a remarkably consistent, stable genre, both in terms of its readership (still one of those most universally popular) and what its audience wants.

This is a good and a bad thing. Good, because it means that the romance novelist can really target her writing to a large but defined market. Bad, because an author could be lulled into a false sense of security based on a generalized perception about what's wanted and lose the very thing that matters most: her unique voice. It is very tempting to think you just need to write to a formula—the very notion with which those of us in the romance industry are beaten around the head on a daily basis by our detractors, and which romance readers *hate*!

Romance readers know what they want, and as an author you need to know what those expectations are and meet them. I will talk about the key six here. But do take my advice on board with this caveat: use it as your starting point; it's your choice what you write and how you meet readers' needs. Above all, be yourself; write from the heart.

Because this is what a reader of romance craves most—to hear that special voice of yours as they turn the pages, bringing to life the elements that they love and look for, but in an original, different, and memorable way.

Before we launch into the big six, let's just pin down what the romance market is and what it looks like.

The publishing industry divides the romance genre into two sectors: category and mainstream. Category romances are also known as series romances, and are usually written to a specified length, a defined promise and prescribed level of sensuality, and are packaged in a strongly branded way. Mainstream novels are often referred to as single titles; as that title implies, the story stands alone. Generally, they are longer and give the writer freedom to explore, allowing for more characters, a level of sensuality that fits the story and sub-plot development.

Both category and mainstream can be broken down into sub-genres; for example, contemporary, historical, western, paranormal, and erotica, to name but a few.

And, though the approaches to writing for one or the other are perhaps different, readers of both category and mainstream have very clear expectations.

Expectation One: *escapism.* The romance reader wants to be entertained, carried away, to be uplifted. Picture the women you know; my guess is that they're all multi-taskers, living too-hectic lives, doing incredible juggling acts to keep family, friends, and companies happy and functioning. And sometimes things just don't turn out well, no matter how hard we all try. It's a no-brainer that reading romance offers respite and relaxation, a chance to dream and indulge in what might be and see that result in a satisfying completion or an unashamed, full-on happy ending.

So there has to be at least a touch of fantasy in a romance novel, maybe more depending on the sub-genre you're aiming for. Make it your business to find out what the women around you see as their ultimate escape fantasy, the kind of guy they'd like to do it with, the kind of loving they would like to receive from him... and anything else that strikes you as bringing that little sprinkling of magic.

Expectation Two: *the romantic relationship must be at the heart of the story.* Lest that seem like an obvious statement, you would be surprised at how many writers don't make it so; they get diverted by minor characters or plot threads and the central relationship becomes a hurried, shadowy affair, crowded out by other concerns. So, the advice here is short and sweet: take care to keep your focus on the romance from the first page, and on every page thereafter; it's of the utmost importance to the reader to have a strong and developing emotional connection at the core of the novel.

Expectation Three: *characters who engage the reader's imagination.* I learned early on in my romance apprenticeship that readers need the heroine to be their gateway to the story—they want to experience the romance through her eyes—and that they want to fall in love with the hero. Therefore, you as the writer should be walking the miles in your heroine's shoes; step into her skin, see the world through her eyes and your reader will too. She's got to be empathetic and likeable, so whether she's strong, sexy and saucy, or gentle, reflective and building her self-esteem, she's also positive, determined, and loyal.

As for your hero, it's helpful if you can fall in love with him yourself first—and then be prepared to share your fantasy. In every survey of readers, Alpha males still rule the roost; there's something irresistible about a man who conducts life on his own terms. But Alpha doesn't necessarily mean domineering or macho. The flawed man or the bad boy are just two kinds; an Alpha can also be the guy next door—so long as he's as strong and sexy as your heroine, a rock she can depend on, with grit, charisma, and a code of honor that will see him through challenging times.

Expectation Four: *a believable plot.* Fantasy means that anything can happen—right? Ultimately, yes. But how the hero and heroine make the journey to their happy ending has to be rooted in reality for the reader to engage and stay engaged. Readers want to see their own experiences and situations mirrored, the universal emotional truths that shape their real-life relationships worked though and then spun off into the correct resolution, courtesy of a convincing, well-executed storyline. In the business, it's known as believable world building, and its key is using characterisation and emotion to lead and generate, rather than always letting the plot dictate what comes next.

In romance plotlines, you may find yourself revisiting familiar scenarios; that's okay. Human relationships tend to worry at the same things. However, don't be tempted to give a conservative or copycat makeover to a well-used situation; push yourself to think of those unique twists and turns, those unexpected solutions that will make your story original and exciting.

Expectation Five: *conflict*. Of all the elements in a romance novel, in my experience writers struggle with this one the most. It's a scary word, conflict; it conjures up thoughts of bad emotions like anger and revenge, and we want everything in our fantasy romance gardens to be rosy, don't we? Again, ultimately we do. But the road to that destination needs to be a little rough, because that's how reality is, and it makes for a much more enjoyable story. Conflict adds suspense and tension—that delicious feeling of anticipation as the reader turns the pages, wondering what will happen next.

Creating good conflict is an art. Too much of it in a story is uncomfortable, exhausting, and boring; too little is uncomfortable, dull, and boring. Look to your main characters and their emotions in order to build and grow the conflict between them. What's keeping them apart? What are the personal inner struggles that they bring to the relationship, and that create barriers? What are the motivations that divide or unite? How much does their sexual attraction cause sparks? How do your characters manifest and resolve their conflicts—by action or discussion? Think of conflict like an ocean tide; it ebbs and flows, comes in and goes out, and is driven by the emotional weather, as to whether things are stormy or calm.

Expectation Six: *sensual content*. Romance and sensuality go hand in hand. However, the amount of sensuality in a romance novel can vary a great deal. Indeed, the market segments itself partly on the level of sexual content and explicitness. Some readers enjoy just a little, some like more but want it delivered slow and seductive, and there are others who want it fast and hot, frequent, and descriptive.

There's nothing worse than bad sex! Thus, you must be honest with yourself and write only what you feel comfortable with. Also, never look on sex as an element that has to be inserted (if you'll pardon the pun) at set intervals. It has to fit your characters and be part and parcel of the plot. Look to the developing relationship to define and drive how the sex occurs, its level of steaminess and its role in supporting the expression of emotion. Make sure that your love scenes move the story forward, and aren't just there for a quick thrill!

Be mindful, too, of how women relate to sex and use it as an emotional expression. There are times when they, too, just want a no-strings affair. But mostly, closeness, intimacy, faithfulness, and consideration are big incentives. How it feels matters more than how it looks.

That's a great maxim for writing romance generally: how it feels matters more than how it looks. So, when you're ready to write, know what readers' key expectations are, but do also remind yourself of that caveat we discussed earlier: *above all, be yourself; write from the heart.*

Good luck!

Ready, Set, Go

by Jane Porter

Ready: Attitude Is Everything

Before the first sale, after the fifth sale, before the editor or agent appointment, after the worst review... attitude makes or breaks a writer.

I'm not a Pollyanna. I'm incredibly impatient, impulsive, emotional, irrational, and irritable. And those are my good points. But with that said, I've learned to hang tough. I write those words to my friends struggling to sell, struggling to believe, struggling to hang in there, and I don't write it lightly, and I never say it carelessly. But if we want to make it, we have to dig in, hang on, and hang tight.

Some writers sell easily. Some writers write easily. And there are those of us who have to claw our way to the top... and I don't mean by clawing over each other, but by clawing up, like a rock climber, hand over fist, inching our way up the impossible vertical slope, grappling with the cliff as though our life depended on it. And in a way, our lives do depend on it, our writing lives.

We as writers have to be willing to take risks. We have to be willing to strike out on our own. We have to write what we hear in our heads (yes, those little voices are real and

18

valuable). We have to write what we believe in our hearts. And we have to write all of this and make it true, make it beautiful, and make it fit the publishing parameters.

That's right. We are artists *and* businesswomen, and in our line of work we can't separate the two, because frankly, we're not writing for vanity press. We're writing to sell. Most of us want to make money writing. We want careers as writers and we want to find our right niche.

Climbing the vertical slope to publishing can be miserable. It's exhausting, physically and emotionally. It's challenging. It's disappointing. So pick your climbing partners carefully. My real writer friends are all smart and funny, tough, honest, and more than a little gritty. They want to write and they want to succeed and they won't accept no. Rejection isn't going to be tolerated. A rejection becomes a fresh challenge, a new perspective. It's the opportunity for growth, the opportunity to learn, the opportunity to succeed.

I don't know one serious writer who doesn't get bummed out or burned out. But the serious writer doesn't walk away from the craft or the challenge. The serious writer reaches deep inside, finds the courage, renews the vision, and taps into the heart. We write romance because we believe in the spirit of man and the miracle of love. We write romance because we understand what it is to struggle and we relish victory after a hard-fought battle. We write romance because we crave happy endings.

If our heroes and heroines can win, so can we. If our heroes and heroines deserve happiness, so do we. If our heroes and heroines persevere, so shall we.

Success can be defined in many ways, but we're all successful if we refuse to quit, refuse to fail, refuse to accept second best. Attitude in this business is everything. Those who look forward, those who challenge themselves, those who don't make excuses, those who believe, will succeed.

Surround yourself with positive friends. Turn a deaf ear to the doubters and naysayers. Ignore dismal market statistics (the market is always tight!). Throw away painful rejection letters or contest critiques. Delete emails that hurt. Get off loops that undermine your confidence. In short, be your own best friend. Protect yourself, nurture your dream, focus your energy.

It took me over thirteen years, thirteen rejected books, with thirty-something rejection letters before I finally got my first sale. A month later, I had a second sale, and two months after that, a third. They were all new books, the second two written between February and May when I tapped my reservoir of courage and pounded out those new books by writing, writing, writing.

Where did I get all that confidence? Thirteen years writing, thirteen rejected books, and thirty something rejection letters. I've learned to turn the rejections into challenges, view returned manuscript as a tool to growth, consider my decade-plus of writing as a "graduate romance writing school" and pat myself on the back for keeping at it. The more it seemed I wouldn't sell, the more confident I became that I would. Why? Because I've become tough, and I've learned to keep going.

Remember that nothing in this business is more critical than attitude. Hard work pays off. Positive thinking is essential, as is sheer grit. Don't ever give up. Don't quit. Don't stop believing in yourself. Real writers hang tough.

Set: Goal-Setting

Some authors are extremely creative, and others are very versatile, blessed with a voice that allows the author to consider a wide range of writing possibilities and opportunities. These gifted authors can be prolific because they can move between styles and genres, building a readership in several markets. I think this is smart in terms of career longevity, provided one doesn't burn out, but I don't recommend that newer writers do this. I encourage new writers to discipline themselves to one style, one genre initially, at least until a book is completed or a contract offered.

It's easy to get distracted in publishing. There are so many changes and opportunities that if you're not careful, you could end up spending more time jumping between projects and opportunities than getting an actual book completed and published.

Not to sound harsh, but by far the best craft lessons are learned through finishing a book, and doing the necessary revisions to make it saleable. Starting a book is easy. Anyone can start a book. Not anyone can finish it. Finishing a book is hard. Writing to the end is far more difficult than just setting out. So get good at one thing—very, very good—before you stretch yourself to more.

Something I learned from the wonderful, inspiring Debbie Macomber, was to set goals.

I am going to encourage you to set goals, too. It will make a difference in your career. It will ensure that you have a clear direction.

So on a piece of paper, write down three numbers.

1.

2.

3.

These numbers are for your goals—immediate, short term, and long term.

For #1, take a moment now and write down something to be accomplished within the week or month. This becomes your Immediate Goal

For #2, think about something you want achieve within the next six to twelve months. This becomes your Short-term Goal.

For #3, think about where you'd like to be in five years. Keep it somewhat realistic so you have a shot at achieving it. Write this down. It's your Long-term Goal.

Save these goals. Put them somewhere you can see them, perhaps on your writing bulletin board, or put them in your wallet. I keep goals posted, and periodically check my goals. It's amazing what I've done, and where clear goal-setting has taken me.

I truly believe that if you're focused about what you want to achieve, and work hard at writing smart and writing well, you can accomplish great things.

Good luck, stay focused, and get writing!

Go: Kickstarting That Book

Every author contributing to this book is a seasoned writer with some serious writing chops, and each one of us wraps up a book and needs to jump into the next. Most of us write three to five books a year (or more!) and we don't have the luxury of brainstorming over weeks or months. We need to focus, make decisions, and get going.

So how does one kickstart a manuscript when time's short, or energy's low? How to take that little spark of an idea, and make it sustain an entire book?

First: Make Sure Your Characters Have Sufficient Motivation

Writing a book without motivated characters is asking for trouble. Characters that lack clear, strong goals—and goals in opposition to each other—will drag your plot, and pacing way, way down. To write fast, to write tight, compelling scenes, your characters need to want something, and not 'down the road', but immediately. They need goals that are going to be foremost in their thoughts, burning strong within them. If you're not sure about the goal and motivation thing, grab Debra Dixon's book, *GMC: Goal, Motivation and Conflict*, and study up!

Second: Choose Characters, A Setting, Or Time Period That Interests You

We've all tried to sludge our way through stories that don't grip us. So don't write a story you're not crazy about. And if your characters seem just so-so, what would make you really love them? What would make you fall in love with your plot? Think about the fire you like in a heroine, the strength or humor in a hero, think about the tone or sensuality you respond to when reading a book. Give this life, this vitality, to your new project. Sometimes we decide we'll save the 'great idea' for the next book, or a book in the future, but pour your heart into this book because it is your future.

Third: Change What's Bogging You Down

If you find you can't write at your desktop lately, get out of the house. Use a notepad, your Alphasmart (my Alphasmart is my savior!), laptop—whatever you need to put you in a different place, away from your ordinary distractions. If you feel too sleepy—add an extra cup of coffee, go for a walk, play lively music—whatever it takes to jumpstart you.

If you find you can't concentrate, or tend to daydream, set a timer, tell yourself that for the next fifteen minutes all you're going to do is write. Just write. No email. No editing. No researching. No fussing with words. Just fresh new stuff. And for ten minutes, or fifteen minutes—do it. I can almost guarantee that by the end of the ten or fifteen minutes, you'll be in the groove and in the middle of a great scene. The secret really is to not make excuses and to work through the mental block. Successful authors all share one thing—effort. They really apply themselves. Be nice to yourself, but don't give up. Set some goals and work to attain them.

Fourth: Get Inspired

For inspiration—and we all need it—play some powerful music, read one of the books on your keeper shelf, watch a classic film, head out to Mother Nature and walk, hike, or sit and breathe in the fresh air. The key thing is finding something that will charge you... fill up the emotional and spiritual well. Sometimes I just need to be with my kids and play. A trip to the park, a hike in the woods, gathering leaves of different colors. Take care of you.

Tips On Getting Going

By Anne Gracie and Melissa McClone

Every author is different, and every book is different for every author. So there isn't just one way to start a book, there are many options. For many of us, we go back and fix the beginning after we've finished the book. Others can't move forward in their story until the beginning is just right, so when starting a new book proves difficult, try one of these suggestions:

1) Open the story at the point where the heroine's life has changed—where some sort of disaster has hit and she's thrown out of her usual life or routine.

Here are two examples of openings from Montana Born Books' Rodeo novellas that illustrate this method:

"She was exactly the kind of trouble he didn't need.

Jasper Flint could see the woman from halfway down the block, like a shot of bright color against the weathered old brick of his newest acquisition. She hadn't been there earlier when he'd left the railway depot earlier that morning for a run around the outskirts of Marietta, Montana, his brand new home."

-Tempt Me, Cowboy by Megan Crane

This opening is from the hero's POV (point of view), but it doesn't matter. The same thing applies, regardless of the gender or the POV character in your opening. Here, we learn that he's moved to a new town. But that's not what's changed in this passage. It's the appearance of a woman that tells Jasper something is different about this morning. She wasn't there when he left on his run, but she's there now. He doesn't know why or who she is, but he will soon, and his life will never be the same.

"A lot of people believe you can't keep a secret in a small town, but that simply wasn't true. Sage Carrigan was only twenty-nine years old and already had two that would blow the minds of her sisters and her father and the girlfriends who thought they knew every little thing about her.

And one of those secrets was just now stepping into her chocolate shop.

Sage stepped behind the counter, needing something solid to lean on. It was really him, Dawson O'Dell, her biggest secret, her biggest mistake... her biggest weakness."

-Promise Me, Cowboy by CJ Carmichael

This opening shows Sage at the point of a big change. She's been keeping secrets, but now one of those secrets, a man from her past who turns out to be the hero, has entered her shop. Her reaction tells the reader his showing up is not expected nor is the visit welcome. Like Jasper in the example above, Sage's life will never be the same, no matter how hard she tries.

2) Throw your hero and heroine together and just write dialogue—go back and flesh it out later, when you're more confident, and comfortable, with how you want to start.

To show you how this method works, here is the first draft of a part from the opening scene of a new novella Melissa is writing for Tule's Holiday Imprint.

"Thank you." Addie hoped he understood the depth of her gratitude. "I owe you big time for marrying me. If you hadn't..."

"Thank you." He smiled. "Without marrying you, I'd be looking for a new job."

"I'd be homeless."

"You win."

"We both win, and get a free honeymoon out of the deal."

"True that. We're the winners."

"I like the sound of that." After losing her home to her family, she'd felt like a loser. "Where to next?"

"Home to finish packing our overnight bags, have dinner, then head to the airport."

"I still can't believe we won a honeymoon in Fiji."

This is stream of consciousness, just-get-it-on-the-page dialogue I wrote without tags or emotion. Although this is still very much a work-in-progress, I'm sharing the second draft of the passage so you can see how this draft method might work for you.

"Thank you." Addie hoped he understood the depth of her gratitude. A week ago, she'd slept on the welcome mat in front of Emily's front door, waiting for her friend to return from a date. "I owe you big time."

"Thank you." He flashed her a charming smile, one that sent female hearts aflutter, brought women to their knees at bars and clubs, and convinced Addie to accept his marriage of convenience proposal. Not that saying yes took much convincing. Desperation had a way of making a person see the brighter side to any option, including marrying her closest guy

26

friend. Sure beat living on the streets. "Without legal proof I was a one woman guy, I'd be looking for a new job."

"I'd be homeless."

He winked. "You win."

"We both win, and get a free honeymoon out of the deal."

"True that." He opened the truck's passenger door. "Here's to fun and being each other's good luck charm."

"I like the sound of that." For years her luck had been bad. "Where to next?"

"Home to finish packing our overnight bags, have dinner, then head to the airport."

"I still can't believe we won a honeymoon in Fiji."

3) Write an opening scene, and then move on.

You're going to end up revising that first scene anyway so why worry about it now? This works well if you're a linear writer and prefer having something on paper or screen so you can move forward.

This is the method Melissa used when she started writing a story called *Rescued by the Magic of Christmas*. She knew what came after this opening scene, but she wanted to get something down before she went on to that next one.

Here's what she came up with initially and to show you how much it changed over the course of writing the complete manuscript, we're including the subsequent drafts of the opener. No matter how perfect you think that opening is, everything is subject to revision once you get deeper into the story.

First Draft

This is the initial opening when Melissa came up with the idea for this story:

"Due to the conditions out there, today's mission is on standby," Chuck Williams, the rescue leader stated at the 0600 morning briefing in the Wy'east ski resort's day lodge. Tape cordoned off the base of the search and rescue (SAR) operation from the rest of the cafeteria, empty now except for the rescue, communications and logistics personnel. In a couple of hours, however, the place would be packed with skiers ready to hit the slopes in spite of the falling snow outside. "We're going to have to wait to bring them home."

Them?

Matt Porter pressed his lips together. Nick Bishop and Iain Garfield were not two strangers lost on Mount Hood. They were two of the strongest climbers who lived in Hood Village. Both were friends.

Melissa's note: "This opening gave me a place to start so I could move on to what happened next. That scene was clearer in my mind. As for the opener itself, it set the stage and gave some useful information, but didn't really get any emotion in there. Plus the hero, Matt Porter, comes in too late."

Second Draft

Standing outside Timberline Lodge on Mount Hood, Matt Porter checked his pack. The freezing mist froze a layer of ice on his parka's sleeve, but he ignored it. He'd look like a walking Popsicle by the time he was finished if these conditions continued.

Melissa's note: "I decided to try opening the book outside on this draft. But I didn't really like how it came out."

Third Draft

Inside the Wy'East day lodge on Mount Hood, Matt Porter double-checked the gear in his pack.

The carabiners on his climbing harness rattled. The familiar clank of metal against metal usually comforted him, but not this morning.

Other members of the mountain rescue unit sat at cafeteria tables and packed their equipment, their faces tight and their voices low. Yawning reporters, not used to being up before the sun, grabbed quick interviews between sips of coffee. Eager photographers snapped pictures of the mission preparations.

Melissa's note: "I decided to take the scene back inside. I spoke with a member of Portland Mountain Rescue between writing the second and third drafts. I liked this one better. I thought the details set the scene well. But I didn't think the opening was strong enough yet."

Fourth Draft

Matt Porter double-checked the gear in his pack, his motions driven by habit and a sharp sense of purpose. Bivy Sack. Avalanche transceiver. Probe. Shovel.

His friends were somewhere up on Mount Hood in the middle of one of the worst weather systems to ever hit the Cascades in December. And Matt was going after them.

Carabiners rattled as he closed the pack. Now came the hard part... waiting.

Melissa's note: "I wanted to tighten the opening and get some emotion in there with this draft. I was very pleased how it came out and thought I was good to go, but I wasn't."

Final Draft

Jake Porter double-checked the gear in his pack, his motions driven by habit and a sharp sense of purpose. Bivy sack. Avalanche transceiver. Probe. Shovel.

His friends were somewhere up on Mount Hood in the middle of one of the worst weather systems to ever hit the Cascades in December. And Jake was going after them.

Carabiners rattled as he closed the pack. Now came the hard part... waiting.

Melissa's note: The only change between this and the fourth draft is the hero's name. I'd forgotten I had a Matt in a book that had come out the year before so I changed his name to Jake.

4) Forget about the opening scene.

Write another one and go back to the opening scene when you know what it is you want to set up.

This method works if you're not a linear writer, and it is a good method because chances are you'll be rewriting the opening scene or changing it so why waste too much time if you're not sure what you want at the beginning?

Sometimes when an author writes the first scene of a book, it turns out that isn't the opening at all. By skipping ahead, you may save yourself time by waiting until you know exactly where the book should begin since you've written other scenes and know the characters better.

Writing Exercise

Make some freehand notes—what does the heroine want... and why can't she have it? What's the heroine's problem and how can you show it in the most dramatic way possible? Brainstorm possible scenes—what's the best possible "inciting scene" you can have?

If you've never heard of an "inciting scene," the phrase "inciting incident" might be more familiar if you're a plotter and studied various plot structure methods. "Inciting" refers to the action or event that kicks off or starts the story. It's what makes your hero or heroine step out of the daily routine and either change or take action so you have a story to tell.

Writing Exercise

Here are some fill-in-the blank exercises to help you brainstorm notes that might help you figure out where to start your story.

What does your heroine want?

If you'd like, break this down into two parts—internal and external.

- What does your heroine want that will make her feel good inside? This question will help you brainstorm her internal goal (example: acceptance, respect, unconditional love, and so on.)

- What does your heroine want that's visible? You could take a picture of heroine with the item or doing this (example: a dog, a new job, a home, climbing Mt. Everest, owning her own business.)

Why does your heroine want these things? (This question will give you a peek into her motivation, but remember you're just brainstorming here. Nothing is set so don't get locked into what you write down.)

Why can't she have it? (Answering this question will also help you figure out parts of her character.)

Is someone or something standing in her way? (In a romance, you'll have built-in conflict if the hero is standing in her way.)

Who can help her get what she wants? (In a romance, if it's the hero, you have a reason to keep them together.)

What's the one place your heroine would never go or the one thing she would never do? (Opening your story with a heroine in a place or situation she's uncomfortable with gives you instant conflict and built-in emotion.)

FOCUSING ON CRAFT

Creating Character

by Lilian Darcy

Creating the right characters is one of the most complex and challenging tasks in writing fiction. If the characters in a novel aren't grabbing readers in the right way, then the whole story falls apart. It would be easy to write an entire book on character alone, so this chapter is inevitably going to skimp in some areas. It's not going to be exhaustive or especially systematic. It's an introduction or an overview, and it's held hostage to this particular writer's very personal and individual take on the subject!

But then that's what character is all about—making the people in your story come alive as unique individuals.

Writers create their characters in countless different ways, and—as with many aspects of the writing craft—there's only one meaningful rule: **Do What Works.**

For some, character is their starting point, the first step on the long and complex journey toward completing a novel. Others start with a plot or a situation or a setting, maybe even a line of dialogue or a single scene, and must then craft the right characters to make those other elements of their story work.

Whatever your particular starting point, creating the right characters is crucial if you want to end up with a story that readers will love—because readers are people, and we need to relate to other people when we read. We need to recognize them and root for them, even though they exist only on the page. We need to plug into their emotions.

Most of the time, we want to *like* the characters we're reading about, but we don't want them to be *too* perfect. We want to see ourselves in some of their attitudes and reactions and faults and strengths. We want to feel like they could be our best friends, or ourselves, or if they're the villain of the piece, we want to revel in the gory detail of their awfulness.

So as a writer, how do you do it? How do you create a real, likeable, believable person, purely out of words?

For me, there are two basic approaches. You can create characters with your head, or you can create them with your heart. Some writers have a strong preference for one or the other, while others use a mix of the two.

Creating With Your Head

A quick search of the Internet brings up several different ways of charting personality types, of which perhaps the best known is the Myers-Briggs system, which divides humanity into sixteen different groups. The Enneagram Institute perceives nine basic types. Many psychologists talk about five dimensions to personality that are mixed-and-matched to result in humanity in all its myriad forms.

You can easily use these systems as a starting point for the kind of character you want to create, and some writers find them extremely helpful. Need a hero who is in the military? Myers-Briggs will tell you the personality traits you might expect to find in such a man. Or you can use the system in the opposite way—decide on one of the personality types described, and then see what Myers-Briggs has to say about the likely career or life choices that person will make.

To be honest, I would probably rather cut six acres of lawn with a pair of nail clippers than create characters this way. I would find it far too systematic, unintuitive, and clinical, but that's just me. It's a **Do What Works** thing. It most definitely wouldn't work for me, but I'd never discourage anyone else from using these systems if they help. Many writers find that they do.

Another area in which your head is important is in deciding what you *need* from a particular character in terms of making your story work. For example, let's take your heroine's mother.

If you've already created a heroine who is a distrusting loner, bruised by life and slow to forgive, then a warm, nurturing, wise and beloved mother just a phone call away is probably not going to work for this heroine or for your story, no matter how realistic and appealing the mother is.

Instead, your heroine is going to need a mother who is *unavailable* in some way. Has she died? Is she far more interested in something else than she is in her daughter? Perhaps she's spent her life pursuing a series of short-term relationships, or she's a workaholic professional, and her daughter has never been given the right attention. Is she cold and incapable of love? Does she have a substance abuse problem?

So many choices to make, and this is only a minor character we're talking about. If you tend to create your heroes and heroines from the heart, you may find your minor characters are put together in this more intellectual way.

Creating With Your Heart

This is my personal preference for how to create character—because I am a slave to the **Do What Works** rule, and this is what works for me.

It's a more intuitive approach, based on emotion and imagination. It's messier, definitely, so if you don't like mess, it may not be the approach for you. It's like making a quilt out of a bag of fabric scraps, where you might grab a piece of an old dress, an unwanted scarf, the leftovers from a Halloween costume, and put them all together to create a pleasing whole.

When it's character we're talking about, you might take a woman's laugh that you heard on the street, something your grandmother used to say, and your own sense of unfinished business with your high school boyfriend, put it all together along with a hundred other details, and come up with your heroine.

Your intuition will be hard at work, also, in making sure that your characters balance and push against each other in the right way. If you've created a hero and heroine who both are driven, hard-edged workaholics, then your story is going to unfold very differently from one in which your hero has those same traits while your heroine is a happy-go-lucky flower child.

The important thing to remember is that both stories will work, but they'll be different, they'll do different things, they'll be *about* different things. They'll require different scenes, different moments of change and realization, different sources for conflict.

One warning, though—it's no good using intuition and creating from the heart as an excuse. If your story isn't working because your heroine is just too mousy and weak and timid to engage with the hero or take any kind of action, then arguing, "But that's just how she is, and she's so real to me," isn't good enough. You have to take charge of your intuition and imagination and control them enough to come up with characters that readers will want to spend time with.

Starting Points

If you're new at this, then you might be feeling helpless about character right now, so let's take it back to basics for a moment. In creating a character, your imagination needs to go on a journey. It's likely to be quite a meandering, illogical journey, although some writers are much more direct in managing to get from A to B. Whatever kind of journey it is, though, it'll need a starting point.

Let's create a hero right now, shall we?

Here are some places you could start:

With His Profession

All of us are defined—and shaped or changed—to a certain extent by what we do, and many people would argue that this is more true of men than of women. A multi-millionaire businessman is going to be very different from a working rancher. Different choices and priorities, different lifestyle, different clothes, different schedule, different fears. A uniformed police officer, fire fighter, or military man is going to have different strengths and limitations and problems from those of a doctor or lawyer.

With His Past

Did he grow up in the city or the country? Did he play sports or ride horses? Did he have a happy childhood in a loving family or did he bounce through a series of foster homes? His past has had a huge influence in making him who he is. Does he accept his history, or is he fighting it? How much will his past influence the story you're going to tell in the now?

With His Appearance

Take a look at his hands. Are they rough or smooth? Active or still? Tense or sensual? Take a look at his smile. Does it come often, or is it rare? What is he wearing? Why? Is he comfortable, dressed like that, or does he look like he's in someone else's skin? Does he look like who he is, or is there a contradiction?

With His Breakfast

Okay, no, please, I'm begging you, don't start with this. You hear it so often. "You need to know all about your character. What does he look like? What does he eat for breakfast?" I don't know about you, but I eat different things for breakfast depending on my mood, and when I create a character, if I really know the important things about him or her, then I can answer any detail-oriented question about them and their daily habits that you can come up with, even if I've never thought about it before.

There are much better questions you can ask yourself about your hero than, "What does he eat for breakfast?" Here are just a few of them:

- What is he most proud of?

- When was he the most afraid?

- What has been his biggest sacrifice?

- What's the most important element in his moral code?

- What does he consider his greatest weakness and his greatest strength?

- Who does he love?

Making Them Interesting

There are many amazing ways to create characters so boring you'll put your readers to sleep. Let's not go for that, okay?

Well, unless you're actively shooting for it—which, true, you might be if you're creating your heroine's irritatingly dull ex-boyfriend. Otherwise, you want to make sure you avoid them. You definitely want to avoid them in creating any character you want your reader to root for and love.

Ways to make your characters boring include:

Following them around through every minute of their day.

Readers will trust that your heroine got up in the morning, had a shower, ate breakfast, and commuted to work, you don't have to mention it unless the showering involved a large spider jumping out at her or the commute was interrupted by a hostage crisis in which the hero saved the day.

Making them say everything that real people say.

A lot of human conversation isn't very interesting. There are greeting phrases that we repeat over and over, there's small talk that we make to each other for social reasons, there are practical conversations we have with the people we live with, about timetables and household matters. Don't make your characters have these conversations unless there's a point to them—if the heroine can no longer connect on any meaningful level with her ex, for example, you might show this with an awkward exchange about the weather.

Making them speak and act and feel things in a consistent way *all the time*.

If your heroine is warm and loving in nature, and speaks warmly and lovingly, and behaves warmly and lovingly, and is aglow with warm, loving feelings *all the time* then not only is she going to make us feel sick to our stomachs, she's going to bore us to sobs. Most people are a study in contrasts. We're not always consistent. What we say doesn't necessarily reflect what we feel. What we want doesn't necessarily show in how we act. Those contradictions and contrasts are what make us interesting. Use them in your characters, and they'll come alive, readers will love them, and your story will have bite.

To make your characters interesting, start by doing the opposite of the points above:

Cut into a scene when something starts to happen. Cut out again when the high points are over.

But what if you miss something important that happened before the scene started? You can always refer back to that in a quick flashback or line of narrative. Cutting in and out of scenes so that you hit the high points makes your characters more dynamic, makes their lives more interesting, with a more appealing pace.

Give your characters something interesting to say.

Use humor sometimes, if you can, and if it's appropriate for the mood of your story. Make your hero or heroine fluent or quirky with words. Show their character in how they speak. Are they blunt? Poetic? Emotional? Sarcastic? Thoughtful? Or are they saying the opposite of what they actually feel?

Create contradictions.

Let's go back to our warm, loving heroine. Don't you just hate her already? Wouldn't you love her a lot more if she were outwardly brash and sassy in her behaviour at times, or maybe cynically humorous, but then kept doing these kind, wonderful things without any kind of a fuss?

If your heroine is timid and klutzy, her climbing a precarious tree branch to rescue a kitten is a much more courageous and much more *interesting* action in terms of character and story than if she's the confident, athletic type who climbs trees and rock walls and El Capitan every day.

If she's naturally tidy and organized, then we know something is going on when we see her apartment in a mess and her hair like a bush and then discover she's missed all her appointments.

If she's normally a buttoned-up corporate type but turns into a quivering mess of desire under the hero's touch, then we'll have a much stronger sense of his powerful effect on her than if she'd already been thoroughly at ease with her passionate and sensual side.

You get the point by now. Mix it up a little. Create contrasts and flaws. Give your characters reasons to behave *out of* character, as well as consistent with it.

Using Characters To Power Story

We're getting into some little glints of story now, and you're probably starting to see how vital your characters are in powering that story.

The pacing and page-turning quality of a novel thrives on things like sudden change, intriguing conflict, and roadblocks to what the hero and heroine want, and it should be obvious why the right characters make all of these elements work.

If we don't know or care about who someone is, then we won't care about a sudden change in their lives, or understand why it's important for them. If characters aren't strongly and believably drawn, then the conflict between them won't be strong or believable either. If we don't root for the hero and heroine and feel a connection to them, then how can we care about what they want, or feel for them if they don't get it?

Using Yourself To Understand Your Characters

We're complicated creatures, most of us—yes, even men, although a lot of them would try to convince us that they're simple beings. If we've lived any length of time, if we've had jobs, friends, families, if we've travelled or played sports or studied, interacted with neighbors, teachers, taxi drivers, doctors, then we have an enormous well of experience to draw on when creating character, and sometimes this well of experience goes far beyond the obvious.

Take murder, for example.

Any cold-blooded killers reading this? No? (That's a bit of a relief, really.) But if you're writing romantic suspense, or straight crime fiction, how do you make sense of an act that's so alien to your own experience?

It's not as hard as you'd think. You can easily take small nuggets of experience from your own life and use them as clues in painting a bigger picture. Have you ever done something stupid with money and tried to hide it from a parent, spouse or co-worker? Then you know a little about what it's like to cover up a crime.

Imagine that instead of your eighteen-year-old self working out how she's going to stop her mom from discovering she's just way over-spent on her prom dress, we're talking about a trapped and cunning woman working out how she's going to hide her boss's dead body after she's hit him over the head. The reactions in both cases are the same—feverish calculations, sweating and shaking, the lies she'll have to tell, the sense of waiting for a trap to spring. It's only the cause and the intensity and the consequences that are different.

Life gives us many situations that are similar in essence to what we need for our books, even if the details are smaller or different.

We all know what it's like to feel pain—even if it's just a minor cooking burn or a cut finger. What if the cut was a stab wound, or the burn covered thirty percent of our body?

We all know what it's like to hold fear for a loved one—even if the loved one is just a missing kitten, or a relative going in for surgery. We all know what it's like to strive toward a challenging goal which we doubt we can ever achieve. In your book, it might be the heroine wondering how she's ever going to pay down the mortgage her feckless father left her with, while in life you're looking at your weight loss goal and it seems equally hard to reach.

Your own life and your own emotions, wants, needs, triumphs, and fears are huge resources for you in creating the characters for your novel.

Some Final Thoughts

Trust yourself.

If some of the things I've said here don't resonate for you or don't work for you, then discard them. Other writers and teachers will have other ways of looking at the question of character that may click with you more easily. If you're at or near the beginning of this journey, you'll need to explore a whole lot of different ways of thinking about character, and about every other aspect of your novel, before you'll start to learn how you create and write best.

Remember the only real rule in writing is...

Do what works.

Seriously, it doesn't matter how you do it, it's the end product that counts. If you create character with the throw of dice, using random flash cards, or by examining monkey entrails under the light of the full moon, readers won't care (okay, they'll probably care about the welfare of the monkeys) as long as they love the result.

Be patient.

Creating character—and plot, setting, emotion, conflict and story—isn't a matter of following a simple recipe. It's complicated, and it takes time and practice and effort and care to learn how to do it.

For me, as a writer, however, there's nothing more satisfying than seeing those people come alive on the page as I tell their story. If you work at it, you'll find the same thing.

Writing Great Dialogue

by Jane Porter

Dialogue is conversation. Dialogue is how people meet and form connections.

Dialogue can bind people together or create tremendous conflict and tension.

And depending on the kind of writer you are, dialogue can also make up the biggest chunk of your novel.

I am a fan of dialogue. It's one of my strengths, and one of my favorite tools in my writer skill box, because I know if used properly, dialogue gets readers turning pages. And great dialogue is what helps your readers fall in love with your characters.

So how do you write great, tight dialogue?

It's a two-step process:

- You write.

- And then you edit.

Both processes require making choices, but then, that's what writing is—making decisions, one after the other. If you don't love what you've done, you can fix it. Change it. Rewrite.

Remember, in fiction, we're not trying to create real life. We're trying to create an *impression* of real life.

Dialogue Basics

Dialogue immediately hooks the reader, and can quickly communicate the most essential information about your story.

If crafted well, your dialogue accomplishes many things at one time, including progressing your plot, enhancing pacing, revealing characters and their motivations, and best of all—entertaining your reader!

Writing Dialogue Pointers

- Nothing goes on paper that doesn't have conflict. Every scene should have a point, or a goal. Every time your characters communicate they should be expressing something meaningful... a fact, an emotion, something relevant to motivation or conflict.

- Every scene should heighten the conflict. Every conversation should up the ante.

- Start scenes with brief speeches, and then gradually increase the scene speed and tension (pacing) with tighter dialogue, which makes the emotion crackle and creates more energy. I'm a fan of using sentence fragments when the conversation is very intense. In real life, in heated moments, people interrupt each other frequently—you know the expression, "I can't even get a word in edgewise..."

- Watch all tag lines, eliminating as many as possible. Don't be afraid of writing simple prose, keeping it 'plain,' particularly when your characters are 'heating up.' The tag itself isn't important—the characters' words and emotions are. I like to use *said* more and more because it disappears into the scene, versus calling attention to itself.

- Even better than a dialogue tag, is an action tag.

He shot her a dirty look. "Get lost, Jenny."

Is more interesting than:

"Get lost, Jenny," he said.

- Action tags have three main uses:

    1. Show, rather than tell, what your character is thinking

    2. Impact pacing

    3. Maintain point of view (POV)

- Emotional tags function a lot like action tags, but they reveal the character's emotions instead of actions. Tags can be placed virtually anywhere in the dialogue, but remember the point of tags—they're to force the reader to pause, to draw attention to a physical action or an emotional response.

- The best dialogue rings true. It sounds real. How to get that realistic edge? A couple of things to remember:

    1. Your characters have to be as real as possible. They're not caricatures.

    2. When characters are upset, keep it real. When writing a tense scene, you have to simplify word choice. The more upset people are, the shorter their words, the more abrupt the words and conversation might become.

    3. If you have characters fighting or discovering something painful, reduce the language to the rawest form possible. You want the strongest, clearest language that conveys a punch.

- Which brings me to a huge point: **men and women don't talk alike!**

Deborah Tannen, linguistics professor and author of many books on communication, says:

"For most women, the language of conversation is primarily a language of rapport: a way of

*establishing   connections   and   negotiating
relationships ... For most men, talk is primarily
a means to preserve independence and negotiate
and   maintain   status   in   a   hierarchical   social
order."*

*-You Just Don't Understand: Women and Men in
Conversation, Morrow 1990*

In terms of gender and discourse, there is a very real
difference in how men and women communicate. For
men it's report talk. For women, it's rapport.

Boys connect through action. Girls connect through
words and secrets.

Therefore, make your hero and heroine sound different.
Have them use language differently, too. Remember,
men use speech to communicate authority. Women use
speech to connect. Male/female dialogue is great for
building conflict and tension into scenes.

Men also curse more than women, are frustrated by
speaking, have very brief, clipped conversations with
other men—or people they do not wish to be interacting
with.

- Not only does dialogue differ between men and women,
  but every character in your book should speak
  differently. Check the length of sentences and diction to
  make sure you are true to each character's age,
  background, education, and experience.

- Dialogue is very different before, during, and after love
  scenes: sex allows men to express their emotions, and if
  a man is going to be more communicative, he'll be most
  'in touch with his feelings' following a love scene.

- Use foreign words or phrases to enhance atmosphere or
  setting—try to vary them, be aware of how and when
  you use them, and use them correctly.

Dialogue and Subtext

By Kelly Hunter

One of the best compliments a reader can give an author is, "I like your dialogue." That's because dialogue is one of the key elements of good story. Leslie Wainger, in her *Writing a Romance Novel For Dummies* how-to book, goes so far as to say that, "No matter how beautifully you write narrative, no matter how cleverly you plot, no matter how complex and interesting an emotional conflict you set up, if you can't write dialogue, you can't write a good romance."

So what is dialogue, exactly? And how do we make it engaging?

Dialogue is a conversation between people. Within story, it's a conversation between your characters. But dialogue is not just about what is *said*. Dialogue also covers what is *meant*, the context in which it is given, and how it is interpreted. Good dialogue has layers. And sometimes it helps to unpack those layers just to see who's bringing what to the conversation.

The Literal Layer

Think of this as the top layer if you like. Here we're talking about a straightforward, literal interpretation of the words on the page. A dictionary definition.

For example, in the movie *The King & I (1956)*, the one with Deborah Kerr and Yul Brynner, there's a scene where the King wants Anna and her young son to live within the palace walls. Anna wants a house of her own outside the palace walls.

> *Anna: "Oh, yes, I'm sure we could look out and see many things, such as iron bars and guards at the doors etcetera, etcetera, etcetera."*
>
> *King: "What is this etcetera?"*
>
> *Anna: "Well, it means, and all the rest and so forth, Your Majesty."*

There's plenty going on in this dialogue but one of the things it does beautifully is define the literal meaning of *etcetera* for the viewers.

Beneath the Literal Layer Lies the Subtext

Subtext is the content underneath the spoken dialogue. Under dialogue, there can be conflict, anger, competition, pride, showing off, or other implicit ideas and emotions. Subtext is the meaning behind the words.

One way to break down subtext is to try to determine who's thinking what as the dialogue is being exchanged. What is the hero thinking? What is the heroine thinking? What might other minor characters be thinking? What might the reader be thinking? And does anyone's thinking change over the course of the conversation?

For example, in the film *Romancing The Stone (1984)* starring Kathleen Turner and Michael Douglas, there's a key scene where Joan Wilder and Jack T. Colton have left the jungle, entered a village, and are looking for a car to take them to civilization. Unfriendly locals direct them to the local drug lord's house. They knock on the door and are turned away. They end up surrounded by many bad guys with many guns. They're outnumbered and seemingly out of options. And then, with the muttering of a single line of dialogue, the scene turns.

Jack: "Okay, Joan Wilder, write us out of this one."

Drug lord: "Joan Wilder? The Joan Wilder?" He opens the door. "You are Joan Wilder the novelist?"

Joan: "Yes, I am."

Let's break this gorgeous dialogue down, because, although these lines seem simple, this dialogue works hard.

- The Literal Layer

  Yes, she is indeed Joan Wilder the novelist. At first glance these words aren't particularly revealing or even interesting. There's repetition. It's information that both main characters and the audience already have.

  There's a sneaky joke, in that Joan Wilder has indeed written them out of this predicament—the drug lord offers his hospitality because he reads and enjoys her novels. But that's not the only reason this dialogue is so engaging. There's a *lot* of subtext at work here. Let's break it down into who's thinking what.

- What the Drug Lord Thinks

  The drug lord has a very high opinion of Joan Wilder the novelist. He loves her work. He reads all her books. To him she's successful and someone who should be celebrated. This is the subtext layer he's bringing to the exchange.

- What Joan Thinks

  Joan isn't disputing the literal value of the words. Yes, she is Joan Wilder the novelist. She's in her element when writing love stories from the safety of her apartment.

  Outside that very confined space, however, Joan is timid, introverted, and often inept. She's just spent days trekking through the Colombian jungle, being rescued from one peril after another by a man who considers her a liability. She's completely outside her comfort zone.

But... right this moment, *she* is the one who can rescue them. They're stepping out of the jungle and into a world where Joan Wilder has more value. How much value is up to her. Can she be not so timid? Can she embrace the drug lord's hospitality and get what she needs from him? Who is Joan Wilder, really? Who does she want to be?

When Joan answers, "Yes, I am" (Joan Wilder), she redefines herself. It's a turning point in her journey of self-discovery.

- What Jack Thinks

  "Joan Wilder?"

  Jack is good with this. He knows her by this name. He's not disputing the literal value of the words.

  "*The* Joan Wilder?"

  Hang on, who? Why is there a *The* in front of her name? Why does her name opens doors—even out here in the wilds of Columbia? Who *is* this woman? This is his verbal cue to reassess.

- What the Reader (or in this case, Viewer) Thinks

  The first thing I did when I heard those lines of dialogue was laugh. I wasn't expecting the drug lord to have heard of Joan Wilder or that he would be her biggest fan. I liked the joke and I *loved* that a major plot turning point came from Joan's status as a (romance) novelist. This moment might have worked differently for me than for other viewers because I *am* a romance novelist—for me it was an audacious moment of flat-out-fantasy and I adored it. My second reaction to that dialogue was "Oooh, the power balance between Jack and Joan just got turned on its ear." And then there was envy, great globs of envy, at all the things that itty bitty bit of dialogue had just done.

A film buff, critic, or director might have sat there

thinking that those lines of dialogue were the most unsubtle voicing of story theme they'd ever heard.

Someone completely immersed in the story might not have had many conscious thoughts on story theme or turning points at all. They were probably watching Jack staring at Joan as if she'd suddenly sprouted another head.

Every viewer brings her own thoughts and subtext to that dialogue: thoughts based on world view and experiences, sensibilities, ideologies and politics, ethnicity, occupation, nationality, and other stuff. An author can't predict every last response that a reader will bring to a piece of dialogue. Authors *can* try to predict general responses and decide if that's the response they want.

So that's one way of examining dialogue for subtext. Break it down into who's bringing and taking what from the table. But how do we go about building great subtext into our own stories? Where's an example that shows us, step-by-step, how it's done? I'm heading back to the movie *The King And I*, because there's a phrase is that movie—*etcetera, etcetera*—that gets more and more subtext built into it every time the phrase is uttered. And it gets uttered a lot.

The literal meaning of *etcetera* is established early in the film when lowly governess Anna Leonowens introduces this new phrase to the King of Siam. The King then takes this phrase and he *dances* with it. Watch the film. Stop the film every time someone says *etcetera* and write down what you think is going on underneath the words. Here's what I think happens:

- Initially, the King uses the phrase to show that *he*, of course, can learn from Anna Leonowens these new things. He's setting an example for his children. He wants them to learn from her. This is how it's done.

- The next time the King uses the phrase, he uses it to assert his kingship. The meaning here is that kings cannot be bothered with the minor details of everyday rule. Someone else must deal with the etcetera.

- Soon he begins to use the phrase as a way of transferring decision-making power over to Anna, who *does* know how to deal with the etcetera of a wider world. He is *saying* etcetera, etcetera. What he *means* is, "You take care of it. And do it your way."

- Slowly, the storytellers begin to reinforce the notion that *etcetera* is synonymous with *change*. The King wants change, and invites it into his world. The ability or inability to adapt to change is one of the major story themes and this theme gets built into the word etcetera.

- By the end of the story, the phrase *etcetera, etcetera* has become a verbal place-filler for all the things the King won't say or can't bring himself to contemplate.

- At the end of the movie the word etcetera has enough emotional punch attached (by way of subtext) that it can bring an audience to tears.

Subtext and the Romance Reader

There's one last element of dialogue subtext that I'd like to talk about, and it's specific to the romance genre. Every genre has its conventions and expectations, nuances, and subtleties that may or may not be readily accessible to a non-genre reader.

Jayne Anne Krentz in her 1992 University of Pennsylvania Press Introduction to *Dangerous Men and Adventurous Women: Romance Writers on the Appeal of the Romance* puts it best:

> *"Critics and readers who fail to comprehend the complexity and subtlety of the genre frequently dismiss the books as poorly written or unimaginative, when the simple truth is that they just don't understand the encoded*

information in the text."

Do be aware that there's a great deal of coded dialogue and language available to romance authors and that most romance readers will instinctively understand it. Use it wisely. Embrace it (that's what it's there for). Don't be afraid to layer subtext, and then more subtext, into your dialogue. And have fun.

References:

Romancing The Stone, Twentieth Century Fox (1984)

The King And I, Twentieth Century Fox (1956)

Writing A Romance Novel For Dummies, by Leslie Wainger, John Wiley & Sons, Inc. (2004)

Dangerous Men and Adventurous Women: Writers on the Appeal of the Romance, by Jayne Ann Krentz, University of Pennsylvania Press (September 1, 1992)

Texture and the Marketplace

By Kim Boykin

The Market

You might have found this book because someone, a prospective agent or editor, a fellow writer, or friend has told you that your story lacks something. They tap danced around until the word *texture* came out. Or maybe the word didn't come out. Maybe they just said the story needs something, but they couldn't tell you what it is... just something.

The same thing happened to me after I rewrote a manuscript three times for a prospective editor at Random House. He liked my story, but the last email I got from him before I gave up and moved on said the exact same thing your friends said to you, only he said, "The story needs texture. I can't even tell you what that is, but that's what it needs to make it publishable, marketable."

Worse still, he gave me a laundry list of texture laden books to read, titles I won't mention because I'm extremely ADHD and can't read anything unless I'm interested, and these books didn't interest me. That was over ten years ago. Since then, that editor has become one of the biggest agents in the country, I figured out what the heck texture is, and Penguin published my first novel *The Wisdom of*

Hair.

To understand just how important texture is to your story, let's take a look at the facts of today's fiction market. Really? You're writing the Great American Novel and this chick wants to talk marketing? Yes. As sacred as the creative process is, if you want to publish, whether we're talking traditional or self-publishing you need to understand today's market... unless you have no desire to sell a book ever, and you totally bought this book by accident.

So here's the Cliffs Notes on today's market. More than two-thirds of all fiction sales today are branded. That means when you're cruising your brick and mortar bookstore or you're online looking for your next book to download, you'll plunk down money on the brands, I mean authors, you know. You choose James Patterson, Pat Conroy, Jodi Picoult, just plug in the brand name because that's what you're buying. And why are you buying them? Because you know what you're going to get.

Of course you don't know how the story unfolds, but you choose that author's story because they've taken you to a time and place you wanted to go, gave you a satisfying experience, and you're reasonably sure you can count on them to do that again with that new release. Another interesting fact about fiction sales is even with the decline of brick and mortar stores more than half of all fiction sales come from hand selling and personal recommendations. The latter is due to the importance of book review outlets like Goodreads, Amazon, Barnes & Noble and—make no mistake—readers who are getting ready to spend their mad money on books read those reviews.

When I was a debut novelist, I'll be honest with you. I was told bookstores are dead, don't waste your time marketing. Heck—even the CEO of Barnes and Noble was quoted in a major trade publication, as he was trying to explain their dire straits, as saying their corporate plan predicted books would be dead by now. But nobody sells books better than a bookseller who is in the business for one reason only and it's not to get rich.

These people love books, so when they love your book, when they put it in someone's hands, swoon a little, maybe even get a little misty and say, "Read this," that's powerful stuff. As a matter of fact, I'll take a thousand swooning booksellers at a thousand brick and mortar stores over a guest shot on one of the major network morning shows anytime.

So what is it about these branded books? What do they have that you don't? Well, maybe you do have some of these things, maybe all; at least I hope you do. Characteristics all of these books have in common:

- Memorable characters.

- Readers can't put the book down.

- The story moves and entertains.

- The writer has a unique voice, just like you do.

- Over and above all of these things, they have a great story.

What Makes a Great Story?

Okay we've looked at the market. We know what those authors have that you don't. Or maybe your story does have all of those, but you're still getting rejection letters or your self-published title is going nowhere. The answer is most likely what that editor told me ten years ago, the thing my manuscript needed to get that big YES I've dreamed of my whole life.

Texture!

If you're not pulling your hair out by now, you're probably screaming at the page, and you should be, demanding to know what in the heck texture is. And if you really need to learn how to use it, why isn't there a multitude of writing books to help you out? If someone has written a whole book, or even a half-book of say 40,000 words complete with charts and diagrams and methods to answer this question, and you bought it, you've been had.

Trust me, everything you need to know about texture is in this little lesson, but, like any other writing tool, it's up to you to figure out how to use it. The best analogy I know is that it's like learning how to cook by eyeballing ingredients, by getting the feel of how much is too much, knowing when to say "when." Oh, and one more thing, after you learn what texture is and how to use it, I hope you'll do something important—write with your ears.

I suppose there are some writers, maybe the top tier of that two-thirds, the branded ones we all want to be someday who don't need to hear what they've written, but you do. Trust me, if you don't read your work out loud, I hope you're in a critique group or you have a writing partner who does. It's the best way—as far as I know—the only way to hear your progress. It's the difference between making brownies with flour and water and making them with flour and water and rich Dutch chocolate, toasted walnuts, and pure cane sugar.

But why do you need to hear what you've written, even though you hear it in your head? Because sometimes everything you've written *looks* brilliant except the brownies have catsup and mustard and arsenic, or maybe you didn't get past the flour and water. So write with your ears or listen to someone read your story back to you.

Elements of Texture

Sensory detail

Sensory detail changed my life, or my writing life. I was at a weeklong mountain workshop, which I highly recommend. Even if you can't afford to go away for a week, even if you have a job that doesn't come with a vacation, turn off the TV, stay off the Internet, and for seven days, immerse yourself in your writing. If you're a writer, and of course you are or you wouldn't be reading this, you owe it to yourself.

Anyway, my mountaintop experience came from a wonderful teacher, author Abigail DeWitt, who taught me the power of using sensory detail. Like you, I was missing a huge opportunity to make my writing rich. I had a good story, good characters, and interesting setting, but I wasn't capturing my reader's imagination and heart because I was so worried about pacing, I was neglecting the very things that readers wanted.

Readers buy fiction because they want to go somewhere and they want you to take them there, and the best way to transport them is sensory detail. Now, back to the cooking analogy, you can go overboard or under write with sensory detail. Write with your ears!

Cadence

Another place your ears come in handy is cadence, and if you're a poet turned novelist, you've got a leg up on the rest of us because you already know how to use cadence—varying the length of your sentences for the desired effect. If wolves are chasing your protagonist, long sentences with showy adjectives will bring the chase to a screeching halt. But you can use those long showy sentences when you want the story to stretch out a bit and slow things down. Again this is another tool where your ears come in handy.

Description

This is an easy one, but description is a tool that can get away from you, something you need train yourself to hear, and know when to say "when." The interesting thing is, sometimes what you don't say about a character can be as revealing as what you do, but you have to know your characters intimately.

The Why

Ever been around a two-year-old who asks "why" every five seconds? After you get your story out, after you've used cadence in the right places and what you think are the right amounts of sensory detail, go back over your manuscript and look for the "why" of those details. Why does that character have a scar? Why does the cab smell like a mortuary? Why do her hands feel like sandpaper? Why doesn't the engine sound like it's supposed to? Why doesn't the blood have a metallic taste?

Sometimes the *why* or *why not* of sensory details is more powerful than the device itself. Even if you choose not to use this information in your story, the more you know about "the why" of those powerful details, the more you know more about your characters, and the setting.

Share the Love

Sometimes, we're so worried about writing that amazing protagonist who is going to carry the whole story, we do what amounts to an info dump of texture on the protagonist. Maybe we sprinkle a little on the setting, but that's it.

So I'm going to take you out of the kitchen where our brownie batter is resting and put you on the stage. Well, not really on the stage, behind it, with no curtains, just you watching with a director's eye what's going on with your characters, watching your scene play out.

The stage is your setting of course. What do you notice about it that's different? Use your senses, even if it's the smallest nothing of a town, look at it from the back, walk around to each side. What makes this place different? Find the extraordinary in the ordinary.

You're the director. What do you want to see more of? What could you do with less of? Okay now write that. Add those things to your scene and then read it aloud. Listen for how much is too much, how much is not enough, and if you're not sure, have someone read it for you. If you're having a hard time getting the hang of it with texture and description and cadence, overwrite the crap out of your scene. Add everything little detail you see and then go back and boil it down to its true essence.

Write with your ears.

Plot and Pacing Pointers for Today's Commercial Fiction

by Jane Porter

In the thirteen-plus years it took me to sell my first book, I learned a lot about the craft of writing, and how to develop characters and focus my dialogue, but I continued to struggle with pacing, receiving nice rejections that loved my heroes, and the sexual tension, but editors weren't pleased with my "uneven pacing", or "sagging middle", and so I stopped submitting and spent a year studying my craft. Now pacing is one of my strengths.

So what is pacing?

Pacing is your story speed. It's the rate at which you deliver your story to the reader. Uneven pacing, slow pacing, or overly frantic pacing can confuse your reader, as well as irritate, bore, and turn off the reader.

You don't want to alienate your reader because your story lacks energy, or sags when it should zing.

I know now that I've failed as a writer if a reader picks up my book and puts it down—unfinished. My job is to hook the reader, and get the reader to read, and read relatively *fast* until the very end.

How do I get a reader to rush breathlessly through a book, unable to put it down? I've learned to intensify the story time—the period of time a story encompasses or covers—by varying the pacing of each of the novel's scenes, which includes choosing when, and how, to heighten the tension in each of those scenes.

For readers to read with breathless anticipation, we writers must learn to generate tension within the scenes and the story itself. There's no room to waste in a bestseller, no place for extra words, or slow, meandering scenes. Today's reader is a product of the electronic age... readers want to be sucked in from the beginning, and entertained until the very last page.

So let's take a good hard look at how to pace your commercial fiction novel.

In the Beginning

Avoid opening your romance or commercial fiction novel with your main character sitting around and thinking, or waking from a dream, or falling asleep in a hero's car.

It's a non-dramatic opening and you need a dramatic opening.

Your reader wants action, emotion, conflict, change. Your reader wants your story to open dramatically. That's why she or he has picked up your book. The reader wants to be entertained.

So choose your opening scene carefully. Think about your conflict, and characterization, and how you are going to immerse your reader in your world. A strong, interesting, motivated scene is essential.

Your sequel scene needs to be as strong as your first. Scene and sequel scenes form a rhythm that becomes the pace of your story. So pay attention to how each scene closes, and then the next scene opens. These scenes interlock. They're connected and can increase story speed and energy, or drag your story to a halt. Make sure the end of a scene is setting up the opening of the next, so your reader can continue racing along without having to get dragged through lots of setup for the new scene. The key is to end a scene so that the reader is curious and intrigued by what's happening next, and ready to dive into the new scene.

After the First Three Chapters

Start at the center of the scene.

The beginning of many scenes is really just a preparation for reaching the center of the scene, the place where the important action and emotion will be revealed. The reader doesn't care about the prep stuff—the reader wants the good stuff. The juicy stuff.

- If possible, start as close to the thrust of the action and emotion as possible.

- Keep the stage clean and free of peripheral clutter.

- Keep emotional or sexual tension high by eliminating secondary characters whenever possible, pulling out subplots that don't forward central plot or conflict, and keep dialogue and emotion focused.

Problem Solving

There will be times you need to increase the story's pace, or perhaps slow it down.

Every writer has favorite techniques for creating variety and tension in a manuscript, and these are four of my favorite fixes for a lagging, or non-compelling, story:

- Impose a deadline. There's nothing like the clock ticking to create a sense of urgency. Create a reason that events must happen soon, if not immediately.

- Up the ante. Along with adding time constraints to your dilemma, heighten the stakes. Make the task harder, the challenge larger, the danger greater.

- Create a mystery. Create doubt and uncertainty in the reader's mind—force the reader to ask questions, to want resolution, to need information—which will keep the readers turning pages to discover the answer.

- Swap POV. Scenes dragging, tension lagging? Might be time to change POV. Some authors write scenes from the POV of whatever character has the most to lose. I sometimes change POV just to infuse a scene with new energy... as well as to layer emotion, build tension, and add complexity.

Perfect Pacing

By Nancy Robards Thompson

Have you seen the Broadway production *Stomp*? It's that percussion show where dancers and musicians use garbage cans and pots and pans and PVC pipe and such and somehow bang on them in a way that creates a rhythm that make you say, "Wow! That's cool!" It's just a sound that creates a rhythm that stirs an emotion and pretty soon your foot's tapping along and you've got the head-bob going and you're dancing in your seat.

On the other hand, if I took my ballpoint pen and went Click, Click, Click, Click, you'd probably want to grab the pen out of my hand to stop me from making that monotonous noise.

It's a sound, just like the cast of Stomp was making a sound. But rather than standing up on stage for two hours going Click, Click, Click, Click, they varied the sound—made it fast and slow, loud and soft.

I'm sure right about now you're wondering what the heck this has to do with writing?

A lot.

Pacing is the rhythm of the novel. Just like the artists in *Stomp* incorporate cadences and sounds into an arrangement that makes you tap your foot and snap your fingers, novels have a cadence or rhythm.

Pacing is the arrangement of words into sentences and sentences into paragraphs and how they're woven into scene and sequel to form the chapters in a book. It's also the speed at which events within the novel unfold.

Our words don't emit physical sounds, but on the page the way we weave words and sentences can either stir emotion much like the talent in *Stomp,* or we can be monotonous like the clicking pen and put people to sleep.

Perfect pacing is what evokes that interest and emotional investment that keeps readers and editors turning the page.

Good pacing can often mean the difference between an editor writing that ambiguous, maddening, "I just didn't love it" rejection letter or calling you and uttering those anticipated golden words, "I couldn't put it down. I want to buy that book."

As author and teacher Vicki Hinze says, good pacing is "using specific word choices and sentence structure to tap the emotions of the reader so that she feels what the writer wants the reader to feel at any given time during the story."

Pretty powerful stuff, huh? Sort of sounds like we are the mistresses of our universes, doesn't it?

Well, we are. Let's take a look at some things you can do to create a perfectly paced novel that keeps editors and readers coming back for more.

Ten Tips for Perfect Pacing

1. Get a solid grasp on *scene* and *sequel*. A scene is a unit of drama that contains action and dialogue and moves the story along at a good clip. A sequel is the aftermath that follows. It's generally more meditative or thoughtful and slows the pace.

2. Backstory, introspection, long blocks of narrative, long sentences, softer verbs, and descriptions with layered sensory detail slow the pacing and encourage readers'

minds to linger in the scene.

3. Dialogue and action quicken the pace, as do short, snappy sentences and punchy, active verbs.

4. Pacing that's too slow puts the writer to sleep. But slower pacing can emphasize something or expand the emotional impact. It shows the reader that this is something important and she should pay attention.

5. To feel intensely, you must have a contrast. So after an intense scene, slow the pace so that the reader can reflect on the action that's just happened. Pacing that's too fast leaves the reader exhausted and in turn encourages her put down the book. Give the reader moments of intensity, but also allow her to catch her breath.

6. Use flashbacks sparingly. Flashbacks bring the story's momentum to a screeching halt and, if they go on too long, you run the risk of making it difficult for a reader to reconnect with the story.

7. Every scene should have a purpose. In a romance, each scene should further the romance. Be very picky about what you put in your book Remember, you are the mistress of your universe and you can condense, compress, or expand time.

8. Use transitions to move past the mundane.

9. The French author Gustave Flaubert said to convince a reader that something is important, it must be mentioned three times. For important points, think in threes: Foreshadow the point; reinforce the point; have the character act on the point.

10. Familiarize yourself with the fundamentals of three-act structure (beginning, middle and end); pay special attention to turning points and hooks.

Backstory: Your Characters Can't Live Without It

By Anne McAllister

Your story is what happens between the covers of your book. True or false?

True... and false.

True because the tale you are telling generally begins with your hero or heroine in their ordinary world until an "inciting incident"—a call to action, some say—jars the status quo and makes them respond.

Often that first response is, "No." *No, I don't want to go. No, I don't want to try. No, I don't want to take a risk.*

And then... something else—often something worse—comes along and your hero has no choice. He has to take a leap into this new, often scary, world. He has to get involved in this new challenge, deal with the curves that life throws him in order to grow, in order to win the day, to get the girl.

So, yes, it's true that your story exists between the covers. But there's more to your story than that.

What is the inciting incident? What action is he called to take? Why does it matter so much that he change or do something different now? Why does he want to say no? Why will he ultimately say yes?

Because of what happened before. Before what?

Before Page One

Unless you start your book the day your main characters were born, they don't turn up on page one without some sort of history, some sort of story that brought them to this point. And even if you do start it clear back when they were born, chances are your characters will be burdened with parents, siblings, an environment that is supportive or hostile to their well-being, and a lot of familial expectations they will either choose to live up to or reject. In other words, there is no such thing as a character who is born on page one with a clean slate.

That is good news and bad news if you're a writer.

The good news means you have backstory to work with. Backstory is the stuff that makes your characters who they are on page one—not every little event or choice in their lives, but the things that have happened to make them fearful or distrustful or happy-go-lucky or duty-bound. Their past gives them reason to have a chip on their shoulder or a naïve, sunny smile for everyone they meet.

Knowing your characters means more than knowing their age, hair color, eye color, birthplace, occupation, educational background, and how many siblings they have. Those things may or may not have any bearing on your book at all.

What does have bearing are the unique experiences and values that make your character who he is.

These can come from family background, economic and educational opportunities they share with others. They can come from particular dire events that have befallen your hero before your book starts, ones that have formed how he perceives himself and how he sees his relationship to the world. They can come from temperament and talents. These are different for each person. No one's backstory is identical to another's.

Even twins born in the same family, faced with the same reversal of fortune, will react in entirely different ways. One may get angry, find someone to blame other than himself, decide to marry to replenish his family's coffers. The other may be glad of a chance to prove himself, may decide to leave home, see the world, make his fortune elsewhere.

Knowing what he has already experienced and how he has dealt with it before, what sort of temperament and talents he has, what his strengths and flaws are will allow you to write your character's reactions believably within the covers of your book.

But how do you know about his experiences, his temperament, his talents, strengths and flaws?

You spend time with him. Unless your character's life is an open book, there is no way around this. You need to see him in situations that may never end up in your book. You need to put him on stage or in a boat or up a tree with other characters and watch what he does. You need to listen to what he says, see who he depends on. Who are his friends, his mentors, his enemies? Does he react now and think later? Is he so busy considering his options that the opportunity is gone before he makes up his mind?

What did he react to? What opportunities did he have? Be specific. Get the details. Make him tell all.

You don't just do this with your main character; you do it with all the people that matter. In a romance, at least two people matter, even if you write the story only from one point of view. To the heroine, the hero may be physically appealing but emotionally remote and enigmatic. What's up with him? she may wonder. She's entitled to. You're not. As the writer, you need to know what makes the hero behave the way he does—even if, until the last scene, he never tells anyone but you.

If you're writing a murder mystery, you need to know not only about the background your main character—a detective or an amateur sleuth, perhaps. You need to know some of the backstory of the victim. Was he simply in the wrong place at the wrong time? Why was he killed? And what about the murderer? It's a rare person who murders on a whim. What drove him to it?

All of this is part of the backstory.

You may know a great deal of it as you develop an idea for a book. But you probably don't know everything because characters rarely come fully formed. Discovering a character's backstory is like getting to know a person you've just met. You may feel an affinity for them, a sense of rapport, which is good because if you write about him, chances are you're going to be living inside his skin for a number of months. But when you first meet him, you don't know all there is to know.

Getting to know people, real or fictional, takes time. Most heroes and heroines don't just open their mouths and blurt out everything that's ever happened to them. What's intriguing about them—what makes us want to write about them—is that they usually have secrets. Some are decidedly closed-mouthed and downright perverse when it comes to sharing their inner selves. They tend to protect themselves even from authors who want to give them happy endings (I often wonder about characters in literary fiction who aren't guaranteed a happy ending. What makes them open up? Are they so miserable that they just need to be understood?)

Whatever it is, authors have to be patient with characters determined to play their cards close to their chest. Sometimes, bless their little fictional hearts, they trust you enough to open up a little, to give you clues as to how they ended up on the cliff's edge or at the wedding of their own true love who is about to marry someone else.

But there are also days when your character clams up, turns away, walks out of the room. Often this happens when you're actually writing a scene that has to be in the book.

So it isn't backstory, you say. It's the story you're trying to tell right now, and your characters aren't cooperating!

Why? Because something is hanging them up. Something you don't know about yet. Something they haven't told you.

If a hero's motivation seems thin, if he wants to talk about the weather when you want him to have a heart-to-heart with the heroine, if there seems to be No Good Reason why he should be on walking on the beach at the very moment that he needs to be, you haven't dug deep enough yet.

You still need to discover more. You need to find out what happened the last time he went fishing or the year he went to the senior prom with his best friend's girl or what went wrong with the ex-wife that, until this very moment, you never knew he had.

In other words, the problem is very likely not in your book at all. It's in the backstory that brought him there.

Once you figure out what is compelling him to clam up or to steer your scene in the wrong direction or to pick a fight with the heroine, you can move forward.

Except... how do you do that?

There are probably as many ways as there are writers. Some authors say they simply make up what happens and move on. No problem. In fact, I suspect they haven't really 'made something up' and moved on, but are so deeply in tune with their characters that they instinctively know what has made them tick.

For the rest of us, discovering the backstory that makes our characters' motivations resonate with their actions can be like playing Twenty Questions.

If, for example, on page one your heroine doesn't trust your hero and says something snarky, you need to know what motivates that distrust. Did she have a bad experience—or two or three—with handsome debonair men like the hero? But if she says all manner of dire and disparaging things about him, refuses to even look at him, and does her best to never be left in a room alone with him, well, a couple of anonymous handsome debonair men don't provide enough motivation for her reaction.

It has to have grown out of an intense personal experience with one particular debonair handsome man—this man. There's a good bet these two have a shared backstory that colors both their views.

If you don't know what that history is, you need to find out. So start by throwing out questions or scenarios, suggesting them to your characters one by one. When something resonates, keep digging. Write it down. Take notes. Keep them talking. Let them re-enact the scene for you—from her point of view, then from his. Discovering what happened and, more importantly, how they feel about it, will help you write your current scenes.

More good news—if you understand your character's backstory, you will rarely write the scenes in your actual book feeling as if you are walking on water and don't dare look down. You will have the substance of their experience to help you tell your tale.

And if you ever do get that "walking on water" feeling when you write, you will know that it may not be a problem with your current story, but that something is missing. Is there is something about your characters' pasts that they haven't told you yet?

Go back and dig a little deeper, ask them "what if?" and "then what?" Chances are that in the backstory you will find your character's motivations for what happens in the scenes in your actual book.

So... that's the good news.

Now the bad. It's not really bad so much as it is being stingy with what you say after you have started your book.

What you can't do is tell your readers everything you know. They don't care about the backstory as much as you do. They aren't interested in all your research. They don't want to know about every mistake your hero or heroine made that has brought them to this point. They only want to know those bits that will help them understand what is currently going on.

I know. It isn't fair. You have worked really hard doing research and getting to know your characters. You could fill books with what you know about them, and now I'm telling you that your readers don't have to know everything you know. Life isn't fair. And neither is story-telling. Just get on with it.

A Morsel At A Time

Consider doling out your character's backstory on a 'need to know' basis. It's tempting to just lay it all out there—every word, every detail that you've dragged up from your character's toes. But you run the risk of killing the momentum of your story if you do that. The dreaded 'info-dump' is not your friend. It will bore your readers who are reading for the here-and-now, not for what happened way back when.

You want to provide hints that will help your readers understand a bit of what's motivating your characters. But you want them to keep reading as well. They need to get to know your characters as they would get to know people they encounter in their everyday lives. Gradually. A bit at a time. So you have to hold things back.

Every writer I've discussed this with concurs. British women's fiction writer, Trisha Ashley, for example, says authors need to have the whole backstory in their heads before they write. But when it comes to actually putting it in the book, she advises, "You must distil all this information right down so that you can infuse only the essence of it throughout the novel. Use it as the flavoring, not in big, indigestible nuggets."

In one of her writing workshops, Australian historical romance novelist Anne Gracie, says, "Don't explain. Bleed in small pieces of relevant information... from various sources, and let readers decide what the significance is." Backstory, she says, "is like an iceberg—ninety percent of it doesn't appear in the story."

English romance author, Kate Walker, agrees. "Backstory is

exactly what it says on the tin—what went on at the back of (before) the story I'm telling... The story the reader comes to a romance for is the 'front' story—what is happening right here and now... It is in the present where my hero and heroine work out whatever comes between them. My job as a writer is to sketch in any vital details that explain things— but the important word is *sketch*."

In other words, less is more. Tell your readers just enough to help them make sense of things. Keep your character's secrets until you absolutely have to reveal them. Peel off the layers one at a time. When you impart your character's motives by judicious revelations of their backstory, you allow your readers to experience what your character is experiencing. At the same time, you make readers ask, "What else?" may have happened. And they keep on reading.

Backstory is where your characters come from. It is who they *were*. Your book, the 'front-story'—should show them changing, growing, dealing with the past and moving beyond it—or, depending on the story you tell, being crushed by it.

Whichever you tell, backstory is the source of tension, of conflict, of all the details from which you can make your book compelling. Spend time with your characters' backstory. Mine it for those things that make your hero and heroine who they are. Use it sparingly in your story. Use it well.

Foreshadowing: Hints, Signals and Promises

By Lilian Darcy

Amongst the many writing craft topics that are justifiably covered over and over again—Writing Sexual Tension, Goal/Motivation/Conflict, Creating Characters That Jump Off The Page—there are the occasional topics that you don't see so often. Foreshadowing is one of them.

It's something I find hugely satisfying to do as a writer. It can also be a telling measurement of increasing expertise in craft. As you progress and hone your work, you'll find yourself being able to foreshadow developments in mood, character, and story in more subtle and skillful ways than you would have thought possible a few years earlier—more subtly than some of the examples I've used below.

Maybe some of you are wondering at this point what foreshadowing actually is. Believe me, you already know. As readers or movie and television watchers, we've unconsciously absorbed a huge amount of instinctive understanding in this area.

Think of a sunny beach scene. The water is sparkling. The weather is warm. Everyone is having a great time. Now think of that instantly familiar two-note melody, the theme from the movie *Jaws*.

That's foreshadowing.

Without those two sinister repeated notes, the beach scene would be exactly as it seems—sunny, joyous, unthreatening... and probably boring. The music promises us that something is going to happen, and gives us a strong suggestion that this *something* is not going to be happy.

So why signal the change in mood? Why not just keep everything sunny and nice until the moment the shark attacks? Wouldn't that be more dramatic? Scarier? The viewer would get a complete shock from left field, instead of something he or she has been expecting all along.

For whatever reason, as readers and viewers, we actually *prefer* to be given hints about what's coming. We don't want it fully spelled out, of course, but if it's too sudden and unexpected, we feel that the rug has been pulled from beneath our feet and we don't like it. I think this comes down to an innate human need for and understanding of *story*, and story requires change, a build of suspense or emotion, and increasing complexity of interaction, all of which can be signaled and hinted at by foreshadowing. We don't want to be told exactly what's coming, we just want those tantalizing hints.

So let's think of foreshadowing as *hinting*, *signaling*, or *promising*. It can be wonderfully subtle and intuitive, which makes it very hard to talk about in terms of rules. In fact, it's probably clear by now that I hate anything that smacks of rules in writing—the exception being **Do What Works**—and am not even going to try to create them!

What I will do is simply present some examples of the different areas in which you can use foreshadowing to satisfy your readers and make your story advance more smoothly and successfully. Foreshadowing is something that can really help you out in dealing with tricky things such as avoiding backstory dumps, creating layered characters, and moving your story forward at the right pace.

And I'll use a few headings so we can all kid ourselves that we're approaching this in a systematic way, even though we're really not. Here's the first heading coming up now...

Mood

I've largely covered this in the "Jaws" example. Foreshadowing is valuable in signaling to the reader that the atmosphere of the scene they're currently reading is soon going to change. Using the five senses is really helpful here. We don't have music as a tool, the way movies and television do, but we can still use sound. Imagine your heroine alone in her bright, cheerful kitchen, hearing stealthy footsteps on the concrete path outside her back door. When she looks through the window, she glimpses a fleeting shadow. Moments later, there's the acrid smell of burning in the air as her distraction has left the potatoes to burn.

All of this suggests an immediate change of mood, and does so in a fairly obvious way, but you can use foreshadowing more subtly to hint that a change of mood is going to happen farther along in the story.

Foreshadowing can also promise a change from dark to light. We're at the blackest point in the story, and from somewhere comes a ray of light, in the form of a child's laugh or, to go for the literal, sun breaking through clouds and promising an end to the rain.

Character

As an example here, I'm going to use a plot device in romance fiction that used to be incredibly common and is much less so now, but is still sometimes used well—the Engaged-to-the-Wrong-Man trope. As readers, we're going to know from the start that he's the Wrong Man, because the blurb on the back of the book makes it perfectly clear. What we're interested in is why the heroine ever thought he was the right man, how she discovers that he's not, and what the hero's role is in convincing her.

In other words, there's a fine line for the writer to tread in making this man believably acceptable to the heroine at a certain point in her life, but then horrible enough so it's clear she has to dump him in favor of the hero.

Once again, foreshadowing can come to the rescue, and its use can be quite subtle, for example simply in the way you describe the shape of the Wrong Man's mouth. It tightens as he says a certain phrase, when he should have smiled. Or perhaps you want to focus on the over-meticulous way he brushes lint from his jacket. There are a thousand other possibilities, and they can come down to the choice of one single word over another.

There will be all sorts of characters you may need to do this kind of thing with, not just impossible fiancés, because the reader's perception of a character will often need to change through the course of a book, and characters will equally need to change their perceptions of each other. To make those changes believable, a tiny hint earlier in the book can really help.

Some more examples: We think someone is a nice guy, but then we see him boot the dog out the back door with a kick that's way rougher than it needs to be. We don't find out till much later that he's been physically abusing his wife. We find the hero's sister cold and unwelcoming at first, but then the heroine finds her wiping away unexplained tears and we recognize the author's promise that there's going to be more to this character than meets the eye.

Backstory

This is an area that is rife with problems for beginner writers, and one where foreshadowing can be enormously helpful in avoiding the dumps of biography and backstory that slow the story down just as it's getting started. Here I'm going to use an example from my first Montana Born Books novella, *Marry Me, Cowboy* from The Tule Publishing Group.

I know, using my own stuff. Writers do this quite often and it always comes across as a little arrogant but in truth it's mainly for convenience. Rather than rifling through a dozen books in search of the right example, I'll use one that's easy to find because I wrote it myself.

Here is hero Jamie, thinking about his best friend Chet,

who is about to marry heroine Tegan—at this point in the story Jamie and Tegan can't stand each other—so that she can get a green card and stay legally in the USA to continue her rodeo barrel-racing career. I wanted readers to know that there's more to Chet's backstory than meets the eye, and yet both for plot reasons and to avoid slowing down the story early on, now is not the place to give all the details. So we're in Jamie's point of view...

"*That thing* flashed into Jamie's mind. The thing Chet had hit him with a couple of months ago when he was drunk— well, when they were both drunk, in fact. The thing Jamie didn't like to think about, and that Chet didn't even seem to remember the next morning. Jamie always made his thoughts veer away from it, as he was doing now, not naming it in his head, not assigning it a value.

It probably had nothing to do with his doubts about the wedding, anyhow."

There. Done. Hints, signals and promises, in 87 words that will hopefully make readers curious and give them the right understanding that something is going on, as well as more insight into Jamie himself—that he cares about his friend but he's uncomfortable, and he has doubts about the wedding.

The two big things to remember with backstory are, firstly, that readers don't want to hear it all up front, and secondly, that they will trust you to reveal everything at the right times in the story, as long as you give them the foreshadowing—the hints, signals and promises.

Story

Using minor incidents to foreshadow major events in your story can be a very powerful tool in creating that page-turning quality that readers love, as well as showing how your characters change and grow during the course of the book, and giving the story an over-arching theme—for example, overcoming fear.

A small act of courage early in the story foreshadows a

major act of courage later in the book. A character fails at something early, only to succeed on a much larger scale at a crucial point in the plot.

Some writers do this quite instinctively, others have to plan it at the outline stage. Whatever way your process works, these echoing events in your story can significantly increase its power.

Poetic

It's easy to find examples in literature of this kind of foreshadowing. Think of the huge, overgrown rhododendrons that crowd the driveway of Manderley as the heroine of Daphne du Maurier's classic novel *Rebecca*, approaches her new home for the first time. Even though the rhododendrons themselves are not dangerous, they create an impression of sinister ghosts looming over her future that is fully borne out as the story moves forward. The reader is in no doubt that du Maurier's unnamed heroine is not in for an easy ride as the second Mrs. de Winter.

As a writer, you'll probably relish this kind of thing because it is great fun to do, and you're really exercising your craft muscles. Be careful, though, and don't get too carried away. *Rebecca* is lush, spell-binding and almost suffocating in its effect, as du Maurier fully intends. Your own story may be crushed under the weight of poetic foreshadowing if you do too much of it, especially if your book is at the lighter end of the romance spectrum. The last thing you want is to cram your opening chapters full of poetic omens that aren't borne out by the way the story progresses.

There you go—five areas in which hints, signals, and promises can strengthen your story and enrich your writing. As always, this was only my own personal take on a complex and fascinating element of the story-making craft.

The Importance of Conflict

By CJ Carmichael

Understanding Conflict

Have you ever read a bestselling novel and been annoyed to find basic flaws with the writing, characterization, or research? Why is this book, with so many shortcomings, climbing the charts and finding new readers every day? You can be sure there is a reason—because most books don't become bestsellers by accident. And most of the time that reason boils down to this: conflict.

Conflict is the tool that is used to "hook the reader"—a catch phrase in the industry that means actively engaging the reader in the story. I believe building conflict into your story is the number one skill a writer should learn. And before those skills can be developed, it's important to understand the types of conflict and how they are used in writing fiction.

I believe you can look at conflict from the perspective of your reader in two ways—story problems that tug at heart strings (emotional), and story problems that engage the logical, orderly part of the brain (intellectual).

- **Emotional:** These types of conflict make readers care intensely about the characters. We want to find out more about them. We care what happens to them. We root for them to succeed. You may think this happens because of excellent character development, but when we dig deeper we see that this happens when characters have a gripping internal conflict.

- **Intellectual:** The other primary way to hook readers is to make them curious about where the story is heading, and how the central story problems will be resolved. When a reader's logical brain has been engaged, they are turning the pages to find out what happens next, or to discover the meaning of something that the author hinted at earlier, or to see the ultimate resolution of the central story question.

- **Both:** The very best books will hook readers emotionally *and* intellectually. This should be the goal of all fiction writers when they sit down to do their job each day.

Emotional Conflict Examples

Let's look at some examples to illustrate these points. I've noticed that many bestselling women's fiction novels succeed when the main character's inner conflict causes them to behave in self-destructive ways. The reader is hooked, wanting desperately for the ultimately loveable main character to come to her senses and start fixing her life. For instance, in Sophie Kinsella's, *The Shopaholic*, the main character has a shopping addiction. She's funny and loveable—but her trouble with spending is sending her life on a downward spiral. I couldn't stop reading as I cheered for her to get her act together.

I believe *Fifty Shades of Grey* also fits into this category—the main character keeps making decisions no rational modern woman would make in terms of letting a man control her life (including her sex life). Why? We keep reading to find out what happens. I call these "train-wreck" conflicts, and in order for them to work the writer must also create a lot of sympathy for the character who is making all these wrong decisions.

Another category of conflict is one I refer to as the "please let something good happen soon" hook. This works when the author creates sympathy for the main characters by putting them in a desperate situation, and then keeps making the situation worse and worse. I kept reading *Angela's Ashes* because I cared so much about those starving kids. I wanted desperately for them to be fed a decent meal.

Of course there are many more examples of how to create an emotional conflict with your characters. Your imagination is the only limit.

Intellectual Conflict Examples

For an example of a bestselling book that succeeded on the basis of creating intellectual conflict, I point immediately to Dan Brown's *The Da Vinci Code*. This book was a wonderful puzzle—a treasure hunt for grownups. The reader was willing to overlook cursory characterization, melodramatic cliff-hangers, and unbelievable coincidences because the general premise of the story was just so enticing. Who doesn't want to find the Holy Grail?

Another example of a book with an enticing intellectual conflict was Gillian Flynn's big hit, *Gone Girl*. In this psychological thriller, the reader is hit with several breathtaking twists and turns. Off balance, intrigued, and curious about where the author is taking us, we just kept turning pages... and recommending the book to our friends.

I'm sure you can come up with your own examples, based on books that you really loved. Spending time analyzing how another author managed to hook you into reading their book is always a useful way to improve your own writing.

Defining Conflict

Whether you're talking about emotional or intellectual conflict, the writer's goal is this: *Put the reader in a state of tension as soon as possible... and keep her there.* This state of tension should begin as soon as possible in the beginning of the story, and it should build to a point near the end when the situation becomes the most dire possible—referred to as the *black moment*—until the ultimate point of climax and *resolution*, when the story ends (or in other words, the conflict is resolved.)

At this point you might be excused for thinking that what I'm describing as conflict is really plot. But it isn't. The plot is the road map of major story events that take the reader from the beginning of chapter one to the end of the last chapter. Conflict is a quality that is imbued into your characters and your story that makes them interesting to the reader.

So if conflict puts readers into a state of tension, does this mean that writers of sweet romances and cozy mysteries don't need to worry about including conflict in their story? Absolutely not. Without emotional or intellectual conflict, a book will be dull, characters will seem flat, and books will be forgettable. The author of sweeter, or more wholesome stories, does not need to forget about conflict—she needs to tailor it to her audience. To clarify this point, let me point out a second way to define conflict: *Conflict equals the forces that are preventing your characters from getting what they want.*

In a sense, conflict *is* story. After all, the story begins with the appearance of trouble (conflict) in the life of the hero and heroine and ends with the resolution of that trouble (in the form of a happy ending). When the conflict starts, the story starts. When the conflict ends, the story ends.

Simple, right?

Um. Not always. Lack of conflict is a common weakness in even published manuscripts. If you ever put down a book in the middle of a chapter, or find yourself pushing to keep reading, I can almost guarantee that either the premise does not contain enough potential for developing conflict, or the author has squandered the potential in her initial idea—perhaps by revealing too much, too soon, or by having her characters sacrifice too easily and too quickly, their own self-interest in a particular situation.

Most writers do understand that conflict is essential to writing a page-turner. So what's the problem? Why is injecting conflict into our stories so hard?

Well, I have a theory. The problem is that as people living our lives, we strive to achieve compromise and agreement. We mediate a disagreement between two siblings, we seek compromise solutions for problems that arise at work, we try to see the other side when someone we care about disagrees with us. Generally, we try to be agreeable in order to make life smooth and pleasant.

Unfortunately, when we turn to our writing, we don't transform into different people. We can find ourselves working too hard to have our characters achieve compromise, when we would be better off encouraging them to be strong, to stick to their convictions, to care too deeply about their personal goals to abandon them without a struggle.

As writers, in order to create rich, compelling stories, we must fight this impulse to conciliate! We need to:

- Create stories based on premises that are rich in conflict

- Begin our stories with a dramatic action or event that sets the conflict in motion

- Ensure that at least one of our main characters has an emotional conflict that is preventing them from achieving what they want or need in life

- Concoct plots that feed the conflict—don't douse it

- Build conflict in ever-increasing increments

- Layer conflict for rich, believable stories

- Seek the original while striving for believability

- Finally, we need to resolve the conflict with an emotionally satisfying conclusion.

So let's talk more about how to do all of these.

Choosing a Premise with Conflict Potential

The single most important decision you will make as a writer is choosing which story you want to tell. Why not do yourself a favor and make your next story one that has a lot of potential for conflict? When it comes to romance novels, certain premises have become favorites precisely because they are rich with conflict potential. Let's look at a few favorite premises and analyze them from the perspective of conflict.

- Secret Baby Plot. In the classic secret baby plot, a woman returns to her home town with a child who was fathered by a man who still lives in that town—a man the woman has never been able to forget. Do you see all the conflict possibilities? What will the hero do when he finds out the heroine had his baby and never told him? How will the child react when he finds out who his real father is? Why did the heroine keep the baby secret in the first place? Remember—you can always give a favorite plot premise a twist to make it fresh and original. In *A Little Secret Between Friends,* I wrote about a woman who never allowed herself to consider that the man she slept with one time—not her husband—could be the father of her daughter. In that story, it's the biological father who figures out the truth before anyone else.

- Unplanned Pregnancy. In the classic unplanned pregnancy story, a moment of weakness leads to sexual intimacy between characters before they're emotionally prepared to commit to one another. Again, this is a conflict-rich premise as the story will have to deal with issues like: How will the heroine react when she finds out she's pregnant? How will the hero find out—and what will his reaction be? As the pregnancy proceeds, what will be the effect on their relationship? How will the baby's arrival affect their relationship?

- Opposites Attract. Take any two opposite personality

types—a scientific genius and a pro football player, a playboy and a principal of an all-girls' school, a cowboy and a princess—mix them together, then see what happens. The opportunities for conflict are obvious!

- Reunion Stories. Common, popular romance plots often involve a hero and a heroine with a past. He might have been her first love. Maybe they lost their virginity together. Perhaps they were once married. Yet something drove them apart. These past betrayals, hurts, and secrets will provide rich sources of conflict to the author. But past grievances are not enough. Something new must be introduced to the mix that compounds the problems of the past.

- Murder and Other Crimes. In a mystery, obviously it's the crime to be solved that provides a focal point for conflict. But it's important that the crime matters, and that the reader cares who did it. There are plenty of mysteries out there with zero page-turning quality because the reader simply doesn't care how things turn out.

- Literary Fiction. Yes, conflict is important here, too. Consider *The Kite Runner*—and the terrible guilt that the main character must live with until he finally has his moment of atonement. In this book the author proves to be a master at introducing, building, and layering conflict into his story.

How to Get Your Book Off to a Strong Start

As a reader I love it when I get a sense of conflict from the very first sentence. As a writer, I strive hard to bring this same experience to my readers. The tone of your opening scene should be consistent with the overall tone of the story. So in a mystery, suspense, or adventure story, you may want to begin with an exciting, breath-taking action scene. In a serious drama, however, you may prefer an emotional scene that subtly hints that there is trouble in paradise.

The exact approach you choose will depend on your style and the story you wish to tell. The important thing, though, is to engage the reader quickly, to make her care, to pique her curiosity.

Anyone who has studied popular fiction knows the decision on how and when to begin your story is crucial. Not just because the appeal of the beginning may influence a reader's decision to buy your book, but also because the faster you pull that reader into your story, the more she will enjoy your story and want to buy your next book. (*Oh, I remember that author. She had me hooked at page one.*)

Why, then, do so many writers—again both novice and experienced—choose less than exciting moments to kick off the action? Tell me this doesn't happen—even with published books—and I'll be forced to disagree. Certainly, I know that each time I start a new book, I struggle to find the right way to begin. Often my first impulse is wrong. Often my first approach can be strengthened.

Again, I have my theories about why beginnings are so difficult. We writers fall in love with our characters and with our settings. We want to paint a clear picture of both of them to the reader. Our story is complicated and we don't want to confuse the reader, so we need to explain a little bit of what happened previously. We need to do a little setup first.

These are impulses to resist. To write a captivating beginning we need to understand the following:

- Readers will put up with a little confusion for a while. They will wonder why the heroine has come home after an absence of ten years—but they will be willing to wait a chapter or two to find out the answer. In fact, they will wait even longer if you supply the answer in dribs and drabs.

- Likewise, readers can wait to find out the color of our heroine's hair, her eyes, whether she is thin or tall or wears glasses or not. Each detail should be revealed only when relevant.

- The devil's in the details, but these should be revealed in snippets between the action and reaction of your main plot events. Large chunks of description take too much focus off the developing conflict... which is where your reader's interest naturally gravitates. Remember to feed her interest in your story, to taunt her and tease her. Not to bore and overwhelm her with details, details, details.

The writing of chapter one is the most creative stage in the process of writing a book. Anything is possible at this point... let your imagination run wild. Because whatever opening gambit we choose to start our stories, our options for starting chapter two, and chapter six, and chapter twelve, will be constrained by the decisions we made in chapter one.

So this is our big chance! Let's all start our stories by introducing conflict—the kind that we like to read about; the kind that we hope others like to read about—in a dramatic, exciting way, in chapter one!

Making Conflict Work

As a writer you can look at conflict from two perspectives—the conflict you want your reader to experience (emotional and intellectual) or the conflict you intend your character to experience. In the latter case it's helpful to think of the conflict as being something internal or external to the character.

Internal Sources for Character Conflict

Internal conflict is created when there is incongruence between what a character thinks about herself, her self-worth, what will make her happy, and the reality. Internal conflicts spring from a character's body, mind, and emotions.

- **Body**—the physical body can be a source of conflict in fiction. Suppose your character suffers from a chronic illness, say multiple sclerosis, and fears she will never be able to have children; or your character is recuperating from a serious car accident and is unsure if she will recover sufficiently to achieve her goal of running a marathon. Or your character is about fifty pounds overweight and believes that because of this she'll never get the job in television news that she's always wanted.

- **Mind**—conflict rises in a character's mind when the way she was raised or her core values, are in conflict with her true nature. Let's say your heroine loves to teach, but her family raised her to believe that with her aptitude for sciences she'd be wasting her abilities if she didn't go into medicine. Or say your character longs to go to Paris, but she's been raised to think this would be a frivolous waste of money—she should save to buy a house instead. A character can also end up in conflict when she views certain events or situations in her life in an unnecessarily limiting manner.

- **Emotions**—Say your character was charged with manslaughter after she was in an accident while legally impaired. Now she doesn't believe she deserves any happiness that comes her way. Or your character is a spendthrift and doesn't realize that she is using shopping to hide her own deep loneliness. Or rather than arguing or putting up a fight, your character lets her ex-husband get away with controlling behavior, so that life will be more peaceful for their daughter.

As a writer, you should try to develop characters with some sort of emotional conflict—try to think of something that *you* would find intriguing. Chances are your readers will find it equally compelling.

Conscious Need vs. Unconscious Need

Keep in mind that what a character thinks she needs may not be what her innermost self really does need. When an unconscious need is driving your story, you will end up with a complex character and a truly compelling story. Let's look at our spendthrift introduced in the previous section. She shops incessantly, believing that when she has the perfect wardrobe, makeup, and hairstyle, she'll finally be happy. But what happens when she runs out of money and her creditors threaten bankruptcy? Worse, what happens if she actually does achieve the perfect wardrobe? Looking at her closet full of beautifully matched outfits, she feels just as sad and empty as before. Now what?

As you write her story, or any character's story, part of the process is taking that character to a deeper level of self-understanding. All your main plot points should be devised to test your character. In the process, the character's goals will shift and change. Conflict will become deeper. Our shopaholic thought all she needed to be happy was the perfect sale. But now she realizes it's going to take much, much more...

Bring it Back to Emotions

Whether your character's internal conflict springs from a state of body or mind, your job as writer is to relate all these conflicts to emotion—especially if you're writing romance or women's fiction, because these are genres that focus on people and their relationships. Your goal is to make the reader care, to make her laugh and cry. This can only be achieved when you touch her emotions.

If you review the examples of internal conflict springing from a state of body or mind, you'll see that emotional reactions follow from them all quite naturally. When you're writing, make sure you remember to mine the emotional deposits that can be found in all kinds of internal conflict.

Sexual Attraction

This is often something that pulls our characters together, even as they are facing conflict in other aspects of their relationship. So you might think that sexual attraction provides the opposite of conflict to stories. Which is true— except: it can also produce internal conflict when a character feels it would be unfair, disloyal, or deceptive to act on their attraction. For example, a female character is attracted to the man who is campaigning against her father for Mayor. Not wanting to betray her father, she fights the attraction for as long as she can.

Remember to use sexual attraction for both purposes—to bring characters together, and to test their commitment to their competing goals and objectives.

Exercise

Choose one of your characters:

In one sentence, describe his or her goal at the beginning of your story. What does he or she really want, more than anything else in the world?

Now fast-forward to the end of the story. In one sentence, describe what the character will achieve by the end of your book... it should be different from what your character *thought* she wanted. This represents the resolution of internal conflict.

Example: In my Superromance, *The Dad Next Door*, Gavin Gray thinks he needs to find his daughter's mother to help his daughter get over the loss of her sister. But what he really needs is a woman who is able to love and care deeply for him and his daughter. In this case, that woman is not his daughter's biological mother, but his new neighbor Allison Bennett.

External Sources for Character Conflict

- **People close to the character**. Often conflict can arise from those with the deepest emotional ties to your character—family members, a lover, close friends. Problems arising from someone who is so connected to your character will obviously carry heavy emotional burdens. For example, in my *Coffee Creek, Montana* books I chose to make the matriarch of the family a very controlling and manipulative person. Readers hated her. But she sure created a lot of conflict for my characters, who felt a certain loyalty and love for the woman who raised them.

- **Individuals in society**. Co-workers, a boss, the mother of your child's best friend. Our characters do not have as intense an emotional connection to these people as they do to the ones in the previous category, but these people can still cause serious problems in their lives. For instance, a conflict with her boss could end up with our character losing her job. A conflict with her son's best friend's mother could result in her son being ostracized on the school playground. In crime novels, we see conflicts between victims and criminals, prosecutors and criminal lawyers, cops and serial killers, and so on.

- **Institutions**. Banks, tax departments, the FBI, the justice system. Any institution can theoretically be a source of conflict for a character, given the right situation. Often, however, it is useful to dramatize the institution through a character who personifies the values and position of the institution. Thus, in a novel we will meet the bank manager who rejects our character's loan, the tax agent who finds millions in unpaid taxes in the heroine's father's estate, the crooked FBI agent who threatens our character's security, the judge who unfairly sentences our character to life imprisonment for a crime she didn't commit.

- **Physical environment**. At times the environment itself creates conflict for our character. Roads are slick with snow and ice when our heroine needs to make a fast getaway. The mountain town where she is hiding from a stalker has no cell phone service when she needs to call for help. Major disasters like earthquakes and typhoons will also provide a dramatic source of external conflict—and there are plenty examples of books and movies that use them to good effect.

Choosing the Most Successful External Conflicts

Imagination is the only limit when it comes to dreaming up sources of external conflict for your characters. As you sift through the possibilities open to you and to your story, consider these:

- **Exacerbate your main character's internal conflict**. For example, let's consider the shopaholic. She fills her lonely weekends and nights with power shopping excursions to the local mall. When her Visa bill comes in at an amount that far exceeds the value of her assets, how desperate will she be to keep her job? In this situation, she might take on a task (say, entertaining an out-of-town male client, known to be a real womanizer) that she would otherwise turn down.

- **Put main characters at odds**. All forms of fiction derive a great deal of their energy from putting main characters at odds with one another. Scenes containing characters with opposite goals trying to work together can be very exciting. Certainly if you're writing romance, you don't want your characters dealing privately with their own demons, then coming together in the last chapter for a happy ending.

  Again, using the shopaholic example from above, in a romance it would work well if the womanizing client was actually the hero—a man who just hasn't met the right woman yet. Or a man whose womanizing ways have been much exaggerated.

  So, in a romance book, you want to use conflicts that force your characters to deal with each other... and their differences.

- **Symbolize with a concrete obstacle**. For example, say two characters are at odds about which of them should own an old historic town building. For one character the building represents his family's history and the legacy of his father. For the other character the building represents her only chance to earn a living for her two young children (because it's the perfect location for a day care center).

  In this example, the characters aren't really fighting over the building. He wants to preserve his family's legacy; she wants to earn a living. But the building provides something concrete for them to scrap about.

- **Make them unpredictable.** Solutions to story problems shouldn't be easily apparent—obstacles should seem insurmountable. I like to ask myself, what's the most interesting thing that could happen—and then find a way to make it work.

Exercise

Given the internal conflict you identified in the previous lesson, can you list some external conflicts that will make the situation even tougher on your characters? (If you are writing romance, the conflict should pit hero against heroine in some way.)

Building Dramatic Tension

I've read lots of books (and I'll bet you have as well) that begin with an intriguing story, problem, or scenario, but after a few chapters, suddenly fall flat. Why does this happen—and how can you prevent this from happening in your writing?

If we could take the pulse of a compelling page-turner, the way we can chart the human heart rate, we would see a graph of ever-escalating peaks, each spiking higher than the one before. Interspersed between these peaks would be dips, or lulls in the action.

When it comes to pacing your story—or developing the conflict—it is important to remember that the dramatic value of the conflict must be continually rising. There will be times of reflection, resolution, and fact-gathering in your novel where the dramatic tension is relaxed for a few pages. But generally the tension—the severity of your character's problems—is always on the increase.

This is what is meant by "raising the stakes." Conflict for conflict's sake alone, does not a good story make. This is why writing a book where car chase, followed by kidnapping, followed by shoot-out, followed by dramatic rescue, does not necessarily produce a bestselling novel.

Techniques for Raising Stakes

"Skilled writers know that you're supposed to continually open up your story by creating scenes which lay down—but do not answer— dramatic question."

-Elizabeth George.

There are three main ways an author increases the stakes in her story:

- Add more conflict—internal, external, or both. Introduce a new complication to the situation, force a tighter deadline, give the main character a new handicap (say a broken ankle) or shut down a potential "exit route." The point is to increase the pressure on your main character. To make her—and the reader— sweat. But also, to make sure that the added pressure or conflict arises or is related in some way to the original conflict.

  For an example, consider the heroine whose bank is about to foreclose on her ranch. What if it's winter, and an Arctic front moves in, threatening the lives of her remaining cattle? This would definitely increase the conflict in the story.

- Make the consequences of failure worse. As you get into your story, consider points when it would be effective to put more at risk for your characters. For example, a heroine in a situation where she is on the run would find herself even more at risk if she suddenly finds out she's pregnant.

- Compel the reader to care more. Often a slow reveal of all the facets of your character is a way to add conflict in layers throughout your story. For example, you could choose to wait for the quarter point, or half-way point, to reveal information about your characters that wins additional reader sympathy for their plight. For example, our rancher fighting to keep her land—what if she has an unexpected vulnerability—she's dyslexic and doesn't understand the agreement that the bank requires her to sign, yet too proud to admit this to the hunky bank manager.

Make The Most Of Your Story's "Big" Scenes

Scenes of conflict require more words than other scenes if they're to develop to a satisfying emotional peak. In scenes involving important turning points, revelations, pivotal action, try to:

- Draw out the moment leading up to the pivotal action or revelation. Let the reader savor the anticipation before you deliver the goods.

- Remember to consider the actions and reactions of all the characters in the scene. But don't change point-of-view in order to do this or you will inadvertently diffuse the building tension of the scene.

- Moments of high tension require precise verbs, terse writing, shorter sentences, and shorter paragraphs than usual. Go to one of your favorite suspense novels and re-read the concluding chapters. Compare a page of highly intense conflict with one of the earlier pages in the book. Can you spot the stylistic differences?

- Focusing on small details can be more effective than providing comprehensive, full-blown descriptions. (For example: during a reading-of-the-will scene, rather than describe the library, the clothing of the participants, and so on, focus on one small, telling detail—say the old-fashioned clock sitting on the dead man's desk, which is now stopped since he hasn't wound it...).

- Just as you draw out the moments preceding the pivotal action, so should you exit quickly once the high note has been achieved. If it is necessary to tie up loose ends, do this in another scene, perhaps through a different point-of-view character, or through reflection of the same POV character.

Layering Conflict

Perhaps your head is spinning now with the idea that you will have internal and external conflicts for your main characters, and possibly some for secondary characters as well. How can we keep all these balls in motion, moving main plot and subplots together seamlessly while constantly raising the stakes and building to our final climactic scene (or scenes)? The answer is to build connections throughout your story. And to keep track of those connections, it can be helpful to chart your main plot points before or while you are writing. Let's talk about both of these ideas in more detail.

- **Connections:** Our goal as writers is to make it almost impossible for our characters to achieve their goals. But this does not mean that we throw everything but the kitchen sink at them as a result. The best stories have a cohesiveness that gives the end product definite meaning. Some literary analysts may call this a "theme." For instance, you may write a novel about the redemptive power of love—not an uncommon theme for romance novels. If you don't know the theme of your book yet, don't despair. The theme will evolve naturally... as long as all of your conflicts are connected in some way. In other words, each external conflict must be chosen so that it dovetails with the other conflicts (particularly any internal ones).

To give an example of what I mean by connected conflicts, here is a story idea (not a great story idea, but it gets the point across). In the first draft, I have taken a jumble of ideas and tried to patch them into a story. In the second, I work on establishing connections between all the various conflicts.

Draft One: Story opens with the heroine's father making it clear he expects her to run the family business, which does not appeal to her. Furthermore, he wants her to work with a man she finds very attractive. The man seems attracted to her, too, but then she discovers he has a fear of commitment. Halfway through the book she discovers she carries the gene for Huntington's disease. Knowing this, she tells her lover she won't blame him if he wants to marry someone else.

Draft Two: Story opens with the heroine's father, who suffers from Huntington's disease, making it clear he expects her to run the family business, which does not appeal to her. Furthermore, he wants her to work with a very attractive man. The man seems attracted to her, too, but she worries that his real passion is the business—like her father. Her father is in a hurry for them to marry and produce an heir to the family fortune before he dies. The heroine wants to get tested to see if she carries the Huntington gene herself, before she marries and has children, but her father (in denial that he could have passed on something so terrible to someone he loves) insists that isn't necessary. Nevertheless, the heroine takes the test and discovers that she carries the gene, too. She tells her lover, sure that he will abandon her now. To her surprise, his love is genuine and he stands by her side.

When your conflicts relate to one another, the task of weaving them together into a story happens naturally. This is especially true of subplots. The more the subplot events are connected to the main plot events, the better the entire story structure will stand. If you find your story is disjointed and moving at an uneven pace, look for ways to connect your conflicts.

- **Charting:** An interesting technique for thinking about your next story is to prepare a grid on a large piece of paper with major plot points at the top of the page, using whatever your favorite plotting structure happens to be. I generally include: (1) the opening event, (2) a couple of major turning points, (3) the black moment, (4) climactic action, (5) resolution and (6) denouement, or final tying together of details.

Then running down the left-hand side, list the main characters and their goals—both hero and heroine as well as any secondary characters who have goals, including the antagonist.

For each of your major plot points, make notes about the internal growth of each of your characters. Remember, this is a journey that leads to self-awareness for your characters. They will learn and grow at each stage, but there will be setbacks too (generally happening at the major turning points).

Once you've completed the process for each character, you will end up with the character's emotional journey for the entire book—this should help keep you on track as you move forward with your writing. This chart helps me to weave my story together and makes sure I don't drop any story strands. It's particularly useful for writing a synopsis. But indeed, that is another subject...

Exercise

Try charting your current work-in-progress. Does it help you to see the different layers of conflict running through your story?

Subplots

Another way to add layers to the conflict in your story is to introduce a subplot. While subplots require the same basic structure as your main plot, to be successful they must feed in some way off that main story line. There's no point in having the subplot in your story unless it somehow adds to the emotion and intellectual tension of your reader.

Originality

Striving for originality is a tall order. Thousands of books are published every year—how can one writer possibly come up with original ideas for conflict?

The task to be one-of-a-kind does seem daunting, but we've all run across those books that seem to accomplish the impossible. "What a great idea!" "What an exciting twist!" "I never saw that one coming!" When you make comments like that about a book you're reading, you know the author has managed to achieve the wonderful accomplishment of originality.

Originality is accomplished in the following ways:

Combining ideas in new and exciting ways. Maybe there is a finite number of possible conflicts for you to choose from when writing your story. But when you consider that you can combine conflicts in any number of interesting and unusual ways, the options become almost limitless.

Take a time-honored favorite romance conflict and give it a twist. For instance the Pygmalion story is a favorite among romance readers. An upper class hero takes a lower class heroine and tries to make her over into a more respectable member of society. In the end he succeeds—while falling in love with his "project." To give it a twist, you could try reversing gender roles.

Use current events and cultural trends to give your story a modern spin. For instance, the terrible tsunami that occurred in Asia several years ago has led to some excellent movies and dramatic stories.

Conflict Must Be Believable

Yes, we all want powerful, original conflicts. But they have to make sense to the reader. There needs to be an underlying logic behind every action your characters take. Though it might make our job as writers easier, we cannot just manipulate characters to do exciting things in the hope of adding conflict to our story, unless those actions make sense on some level.

That's not to say that characters always do the smart thing. Perhaps an opposing character will deceive them into making a mistake, or perhaps they are deceiving themselves and make a wrong move as a result.

"Conflict for conflict's sake is meaningless. The reader insists that there is a reason for each new battle. Conflict must be motivated—there must be a reason for your character to strive toward a certain goal." – Swain, *Techniques of the Selling Author.*

For example, I can't read a book where a woman knowingly puts herself into danger... unless the stakes are extremely high. For example, I'd have a hard time sympathizing with a woman who decides to be a surrogate mother... unless her reasons were extremely compelling.

Unfortunately it's all too easy for a writer to sabotage her book by not laying the groundwork that will make her exciting conflict believable to the reader. This happens to me all the time. I get so excited by the new direction I want to take that I forget to ask the most fundamental question: Why would my character do this?

The more unusual, extreme, or dangerous the action you want your character to make, the stronger her motivation needs to be for doing so. Just remember this: Conflict must be believable in order to be effective.

The Black Moment and Resolution

Arriving at the Black Moment

There is a point in every book or movie, when we sense the ending is drawing near, yet an appropriate ending to the story has never seemed more impossible. This is the Black Moment. This is where your readers' hearts are beating the fastest, where they will keep reading into the wee hours, even though they have work the next day, because they simply have to see what happens next.

You want this moment to be incredibly tense, emotional, and interesting. If you've thought about conflict throughout your story, if you've woven the strands together carefully, been interesting and original, your characters will be in despair—and your readers will care. You have an ending planned—but your readers can't guess what it is, or at least, they can't see the way it will all come together.

Through a lot of hard work, you've stretched the tension as tight as possible, and from this point forward, the pace of action is going to speed up as your characters begin the climactic action that will lead them to the resolution of the story.

Climactic Action

Earlier, we talked about the importance of starting your book in the right place—now it's time to talk about endings. Although few prospective buyers read the last chapter of a book before they make their purchasing decision, you can be sure that their decision to buy your next book will rest heavily on how well you concluded your last one.

At this point your characters are facing their ultimate test. Their actions and responses to this test will reveal their true character (the resolution of their internal conflict).

For your climax to have the most impact, you must make sure:

- No easy route to success is available. Part of your job as storyteller is to slowly, but surely, box your characters in until only the hardest, possible choice remains. If they can solve their problems with relative ease, (say a conversation which could have occurred chapters ago) then the reader will feel cheated.

- If there is an easy way out of the quagmire, make sure it would be an affront to the character's principles to take it. Your reader wants to see the characters earn their happy ending. And this means they must act in selfless, brave, principled ways.

- Make sure that the cost of doing the right thing is high. For example: The hero is willing to give up his ranch for the heroine. The heroine will confront her terrible fear of horses in order to save the hero's life.

- The characters' goals—established in our first chapters—might have changed over the course of the story as their self-awareness has developed. This is to be expected. But whatever that final goal, it should be something worthy of the character. No reader is going to be moved by a character whose goal is simply to get rich. So what if she wins a lottery at the end of the book? This is not a lofty goal... no one will care.

- A climax is only effective if the situation has been sufficiently built up. When problems are solved too quickly, even if at great cost to the character, the ending is not as satisfying to the reader. Make sure the reader has full opportunity to feel the struggle.

- The climactic scenes must involve action on the part of your main characters. They should not rely primarily on brave behavior of secondary characters, twists of fate, an uncharacteristic slip-up on the part of an adversary.

- Right before the character gains the upper hand there should be a moment in time when it appears that all hope is gone. Don't rush this moment. The more the character (and the reader) suffer now—the bigger will be the payoff with the final resolution.

Resolution

The final result of your climactic scene may not take up many manuscript pages, but it should be full of emotional energy. In this scene our characters finally receive the payoff for sacrifices made earlier.

Readers want characters to get what they deserve. Evil, cruel, selfish characters are to be punished in accordance with the level of their crimes. Equally, good, brave, unselfish characters need to be rewarded.

Rewards are not necessarily what the characters think they want... but rather what the reader knows they really need. At this point the characters themselves may have already developed the self-awareness to see this distinction too. Or perhaps this awareness will only be fully achieved in this last moment of the book.

At this point in a romance, the hero and heroine have a chance to talk out the resolution of their conflict. This may be an appropriate time for declarations of love and full commitment.

In the most powerful books, authors build up to one action-filled, emotional scene, that resolves all conflicts (remember my earlier advice that conflicts be connected?) both internal and external. Sometimes, however, such a conclusion isn't possible. Where different plot threads need to be resolved separately, the rule of thumb is to tie up secondary conflicts first, leaving the last, most powerful conflicts to the end.

> *"Anyone can deliver a happy ending... an artist gives us the emotion he's promised... but with a rush of unexpected insight..."*
>
> *-Robert McKee, Story*

Voice

by Jane Porter

Defining Voice

Let's get down to the bare bones of voice. I don't think voice is particularly complicated. Voice is you. We have a voice when we speak. Each of us puts words together in a unique way. Some of us speak logically. We're direct. Focused. Assured. Others speak more softly, tentatively, with longer pauses between words and sentences. We might layer in extra adjectives, add more emotion. We might change our style of speaking, depending on those around us. With my five-year-old I'm quite direct. With my husband, more evasive.

We have a similar writing voice. Your writing voice is you on paper. It's the basic storyteller in each of us putting an idea together. You can embellish a voice, strip a voice, but in the end, the voice is what it is. It's who you are, the person shaped by life, fate, personality. And in my mind that's the most exciting part of our writing. Uncovering, and protecting, the authentic voice.

Using Our Voice

We often start writing what we most enjoy reading. "Imitation is the sincerest form of flattery." Writers who fell in love with Kathleen Woodiwiss and *Ashes in the Wind* might have tried to write historical romance first. Conversely, someone who grew reading Harry Potter novels might have attempted urban fantasy, while others who embraced the Twilight series might have tried to write paranormal romances or New Adult.

We also have prototypes embedded in our memories. Certain books strike a resonant chord within us. We can look back to myths, favorite fairy tales, Aesop's fables. Some people like a morality tale. Others want escapism, and all of it is good, and necessary. We can't embrace only one form of literature. First as readers, then as writers, we look for favorites and then stretch our tastes and preferences. We'll seek out the new to add to the tried and true.

Voice Exercise

Take a moment now and get a note pad or sheet of paper.

Write down your favorite fairy tales. Pick at least two or three.

1.

2.

3.

Now, think of at least one favorite myth. Two if possible.

1.

2.

Save these. We're going to come back to them in a moment.

Voice and Personality

Who are you? What makes you different from the next person, the next writer? Where is the unique individual, the soul, in your books?

Each of us has favorite themes in literature, and favorite fairy tales from our childhood, because we are individuals with a unique way of looking at the world, internalizing the external, making facts, details, sensations, and emotions subjective. We could all take the same hero, heroine, plot and write a story, but if you were to compare the stories, they'd be quite different because the style, voice, pacing, tone, and emotional texture would be different.

Just as we all do the physical writing differently—some tweak a book in the first draft from beginning to end, others pour it all out one rough chaotic draft—the essence of a book varies from writer to writer. Your goal isn't to sell a book, but to find a home for your voice and the essence of your writing.

Let's look at the fairy-tales you picked a moment ago.

Think about them for a moment. Scribble down a few key words or phrases about each. Why did you like them? What made them special?

Same for the myth. What about this myth did you like?

We're drawn to certain archetypes, stories, and themes. We don't necessarily write them—but they might influence us more than we first think.

It's vital to establish the *you* before you target your audience. Know your strengths, preferences, even weaknesses as a writer. Know what sets you apart and yet what also ties you to other writers. This knowledge has to be more than genre-specific. Don't merely accept that you are a historical writer, a mystery writer, a thriller writer, or a romance writer.

Voice Versus Style

There is theme. And then there is style. They are not the same, although they touch in points. Theme is the message of your book. Style is the packaging. And voice shapes both, taking a common or popular theme and making it unique.

When we've been writing long enough, and are serious about writing to sell, we start making choices about our books, our themes, and our possible styles. We need to be sensitive to the market, aware and educated about trends or what's selling, or conversely, what's not wildly selling, but we don't want to write to the market... especially if it isn't true to who you are, and what you believe.

Voice and Theme

This is what I learned in the past year: I cannot, and will not, ever be able to please everyone. I am what I am. I like what I like. And when I am what I am, I write my truth—what is most real and relevant to me and these become my themes. Sometimes these themes are conscious choices, other times they emerge in and through the story, but every time I wrap a book up, it's obvious it's a Jane Porter novel.

I first sold by writing for Harlequin Presents, and I still write for them because I love the fantasy. I loved the mythic element and the fairytale qualities to the story. But it's not the frothy fairy tales I'm drawn to.

My favorite fairy tales are *Rapunzel. The Little Match Girl. Beauty and the Beast.* In children's stories I loved the idea of *Heidi*, the struggling *Five Little Peppers*, the Alcott novel, *Jo's Boys*—in short, the orphaned, the disadvantaged, the helpless, hopeless, and their triumph. What myth resonated with me? I loved Daedalus and Icarus and the idea that one could fly, but if you ignored the rules, or pushed too hard, you'd crash and burn.

How does that translate to romance? I like a story that pushes the edge a bit. I like a heroine who isn't necessarily the strong, smart, independent American role model, but the different, the unusual, the creative, the scarred. I like a hero who shatters a heroine from the start. One who shakes her world, rocks her completely and in the end makes her skin fit and her heart whole. My books aren't reality, but they contain pieces of reality and doses of hope.

When I read and write, I like to be surprised, I like to be touched, I like to be entertained and sometimes I like to be shocked. Which really all stems from personality. This is me, Jane. For good or bad, this is who I am, what I like and I am going to embrace it. Finally, my writing can reflect it.

If I let it go on paper—tell a story, develop a theme, the way I want to tell it, I'm writing it in my most natural voice. Accept your strengths and weaknesses, and continue to hone your skills. Be the best at what you do. Whatever your strength is, make the most of it. Play it up. Find a market—a genre, a publishing house, an imprint or line—where your strengths shine and start your career there.

SPECIFICALLY ROMANCE

Make That Beginning Great!

By Trish Morey

"The sex was good.

Surprisingly good.

With a growl Rafe gave himself up to the inevitable and..."

With any luck those short opening lines from *Forced Wife, Royal Love-Child* were enough to grab your attention. Hopefully the rest of this piece will interest you enough to hold it.

And that's exactly what should be your intention when you start your novel. You don't have to start in the midst of a love scene and a lot of times you won't want to or it won't be appropriate for your story. But your opening should still unashamedly drag those readers into the story and aim to keep them there, whether they are judges in a contest you're hoping will give you a high score, editors you're hoping will buy your manuscript, or customers in a book store scanning the shelves with a spare few dollars in their pockets.

So we all need a great beginning. How do we make it happen?

When I started out in this writing gig, many, many moons

ago, and was eager to pick up every bit of how-to advice I could, I heard a lot about needing to establish the who, what, where, why and how of a story as soon as possible. Contest score sheets at that time specifically sought these out and you were marked down if any of the elements were missing. Now, it's true your reader needs to be able to recognise the world in which this story is set—who are the players—where are they and what's at stake, but I believe the risk of planning your openings in purely such mechanical terms is that you can in turn reduce the opening to something that looks like one big information dump. As a result, you'll suck any spontaneity right out of those first few opening paragraphs. For example, here's how those opening lines of *Forced Wife* could have read, if I'd been worried about checking off those five w's as quickly as possible:

"In his Paris apartment, Rafe Lombardi, bastard son to the late King of Montvelatte and who had no chance of becoming king because there were two legitimate sons in line before him, was relaxing in the midst of having great sex with helicopter pilot, Sienna Wainwright. In fact, it was so good, he was about to have great sex with her all over again..."

A great opening? No way. And yet that's what was happening, between whom, and where. So how do we get from a bland, detailed story start that reads like a checklist, to one that will keep your reader turning the pages long into the night when she's promised herself she'll only check out a few pages? It's not rocket science. It's probably not even science. And these ideas are hardly original, but for what it's worth, here are the three critical ingredients I think go into a great beginning in a category romance (in fact, any romance for that matter).

For the first ingredient, we need go no further than ask what it is that readers are looking for when they pick up that book from the shelves (or when that editor picks up a manuscript from slush). It's not a difficult question to answer. They're looking for a reason to keep on reading; a reason to part with their hard-earned cash, whether it's a favourite premise, a dilemma, intriguing dialogue, a confrontation between past lovers, the hint of danger or suspense, or something else entirely that keeps them wanting more. As writers, we call these reasons hooks. So that's the first thing your opening needs.

The Hook: A Dynamic and Intriguing Start

This is your story. This is your baby, and nobody knows your story better than you. And it's not only your job, but your responsibility to launch this baby into the world with as much impact as you can. Nobody can write this for you — that's purely dependent on you and your talents — but you can give yourself the very best chance by taking your story's premise and making the most of it. Let's check out a few examples of some of the different ways you can start and try to draw that reader in.

#1 Revenge was sweet.

His Mistress for a Million kicks off with the theme of the book in one short sentence. We're in the hero's point of view and it's payback time and a reader who likes revenge type stories might wonder — what happened? — and read on.

#2 It was much too late for a social call.

> *"Briar Davenport crossed the entrance hall uneasily, the click of her heels on the dusty terrazzo tiles echoing in the lofty space while a premonition that all was not right in the world played havoc with her nerves.*
>
> *Late night visitors rarely meant good news."*

The Spaniard's Blackmailed Bride begins on a note of suspense. It's late at night, the sound of Briar's heels echoing on those tiles and she has a feeling of uneasiness... so who has come calling? A reader also might wonder why those tiles are dusty in a house with lofty spaces — clearly this is no slum. There are hints of trouble, there is atmosphere, and your reader should be right there looking over the heroine's shoulder when she opens that door, ready for the surprise of her life.

Something else to notice is that we're in the female POV here. Play with that POV—find out which POV has the greatest impact for your own great beginning.

#3 Over my dead body!

Dialogue is a wonderfully effective way to throw the reader into the action and this opening sentence from *His Prisoner in Paradise* lets us know that someone is pretty upset about whatever's planned. Dialogue is immediate. It's powerful and it throws us straight into the emotions at play and therefore straight into the story.

However, the best line in the world doesn't make a great first page or first chapter, and that great opening or wonderful first line is wasted if the author hasn't started the book in the right place. Start the story in the wrong place and despite the best opening paragraph in the world, interest will soon be lost. So what's the very best place to start your story? Of course, it's at the point of change. And that's our second thing you must be sure to do.

Set Your Hook at the Point of Change

We've no doubt all heard that expression—set your hook, or your book, at the point of change. We've probably all got it inscribed on our writerly brains. We know we should do this. What we've also probably all experienced is exactly how hard that is. And even when we think we've nailed it, someone else reads our work and says our story really gets underway in chapter two, or maybe even in chapter three and that everything up to then is really backstory.

Great. So how do you identify that point of change? What if you think you already have your perfect first line? In an extended workshop I do on this topic, I get people to do an exercise at this point, with a given premise, asking for a suggested first paragraphs. As I can't ask you to do that here, I'll relate at bit of my own experience, with my first published book, *The Greek Boss's Demand*.

I thought I'd started this story in the right place. The heroine's boss, Aristos Xenophon, had been killed, she was waiting for a new boss to arrive from Greece—some relative of Aristos. And I had a fantastic first line—"Aristos Xenophon was dead." I loved that first line! I knew it would grab the editor's attention! But clearly I hadn't nailed the point of change.

I spent the next five and a half pages immediately following that line while my heroine drank coffee with her sister, telling her about Aristos's history in Australia, how he'd started out penniless selling tomatoes only to become a property billionaire, how he'd been the most arrogant boss in history but how he'd been taken out by a bullet from a disgruntled tenant—and hey, wasn't it lucky she wasn't there at the time—imagine if her seven year old son had been left motherless!

I got the editor's attention all right. They said, "we really like your story, but, can you do something about the opening—it's kind of static." Surprisingly enough, they didn't want chats over cups of coffee, not even if it was to tell my brilliant backstory. And so eventually I started the book on page six. I cut straight to a scene where we met the hero, reluctantly flying into Sydney and how much all he wants to do is be done with this strange bequest and go home as soon as possible.

So that's why I'm saying, a brilliant first line or first paragraph isn't enough, a hook by itself is good but it isn't enough—it has to be a brilliant opening set at exactly the right time of the story. No cups of tea, no mentors, no kindly sisters offering advice. Don't waste a great opening with a first chapter filled with backstory! Go for the punch. Go for action and the crux of the issue!

Which leads perfectly into the third ingredient all great category romances have—I think the best beginnings pinpoint that point of change and tell it in an intriguing and interesting way, *plus* getting your hero and your heroine together as quickly as possible. And that's something that everyone should already know but is definitely worth repeating:

Get Your Hero and Heroine Together as Soon as Possible

If you send an editor a manuscript that has a great opening hook, starts at that point of change for the characters, and introduces her to them both without delay, then she is going to know that you've studied your craft and are serious about getting published. And she will read on. Forget the backstory, forget the cups of coffee. Get that hero and heroine together on the page.

Clearly, if you're anything like me, getting that opening right is a skill you're going to have to keep on practicing— it's not just a matter of getting down a start, it's not just a matter of settling for something that seems to work okay, it's crafting it to work the right way. Each of my books has been like that—a case of constantly reworking that opening from that first awkward attempt to break into my story to the final draft that an editor approves. It's a matter of working and reworking and it counts for so much at the beginning of your story, so don't just accept your first "great" opening and think that'll do. Keep improving it, making it tighter, giving it more impact and don't settle, until you have your own great beginning!

The Romance Novel's Compelling Heroine

by Jane Porter

Intro Exercise

Before we get going, I want you to do a brief exercise. Think of one of your best friends. Write down her name. Picture her face. Picture the two of you together. Now write down the first three adjectives that come to mind to describe her, and the way you feel about her:

1. Takes Risks
2. Funny
3. Cares about others

Now, think about this friend again. Have you ever had a fight? Has there ever been a point of tension? Think about the tension, the problem. Do you remember what created the problem? When you were frustrated with your friend at that moment, what would you describe as your friends weaknesses? What traits have frustrated you at times about this friend?

1. Bad Decisions
2. Sloppy
3. Late

The rules for men and women in romance novels are quite different.

A hero, particularly your Alpha male, can be very flawed and still admired or adored by the romance reader.

A very flawed heroine can't.

It took me about a couple of years and a number of books under my belt to finally accept the hard truth, that the romance reader—being primarily female—is very hard on the romance heroine.

What made me so exceptional as a writer of great Alphas—flawed, fascinating men—didn't work when I created flawed, fascinating women.

Why? Because for the most part, the die-hard romance reader isn't interested in reading about a flawed woman. For the most part, the die-hard romance reader wants to become the heroine as she reads the romance novel, and she doesn't want to feel too heavy, too awkward, too self-conscious, too foolish. No, the romance reader wants to feel smart, attractive, successful, empowered, and she gets those warm fuzzies through your heroine being smart, attractive, successful, and empowered.

 But at the same time, the romance reader doesn't want a boring heroine. Or a plastic heroine. Or a one dimensional, forgettable heroine.

Quite the contrary, the romance reader wants the heroine to linger in her mind, after the story is over. She wants the heroine to be real and accessible... and as real and accessible as the reader's best friend.

So that's the challenge. Creating the heroine who could be the reader's best friend. Creating a heroine who stands up for the underdog, a heroine who never turns her back on a friend in need, a heroine who can laugh at herself and not take herself too seriously. The unforgettable heroine is essentially the woman we'd all like to be.

The traits of the unforgettable heroine: courage, kindness,

intelligence, humor, spirit, determination, and passion. Other heroine traits:

- The heroine isn't a quitter.

- She refuses to accept second best.

- She understands that life is hard.

- She's always learning, always growing.

- The Alpha heroine uses all of her senses; the Alpha heroine is awake and aware of life.

- She confronts the challenges, whatever the challenges may be.

- And just like the friend you thought about above, the heroine in a romance novel is strong and courageous, real and relatable, hopeful and compassionate.

So as you craft your heroine, remember to keep her real, but she's also a fictional heroine—she must be compelling so your reader, a woman, will enjoy reading about her, and will cheer for her, and be her ally—and on her team—throughout the course of your novel.

Thoughts On Heroines In Romance

by Tessa Shapcott

When I started reading romance as a teenager, heroines of romance fiction were emerging from an age when they had been *nice gels*, as we say in England: prim, virginal, often sheltered and without a profession, though if they did work, it was in a role such as nanny, governess, or companion. It's easy to smile when we think about these heroines of yesteryear, and yet they were important symbols to readers then, personifying certain emotions and fantasies—for instance, the unworldly ugly duckling who emerged a swan, or the young woman who experienced an emotional and (often in a euphemistic way) sexual awakening.

Those of us who are regular romance readers these days know that our heroines have evolved a long, long way since, though at their cores they still retain echoes of their forebears. Some continue to be Cinderellas at heart, but in a wholly contemporary way: they battle with their weight, know about surviving in a lowly job on a minimum wage and dealing with the potential joy or heartbreak that being pregnant and alone can bring. Other heroines operate at the other end of the spectrum: they're city girls negotiating the urban jungles of cosmopolitan international cities and climbing the career ladder, perhaps with just a little sexual experience. They're not looking for Mr. Right, but at heart they're as soft and vulnerable as the next woman, and hoping one day to settle down to marriage and children.

What is important to romance readers today is that heroines reflect their aspirations, emotions, victories, and struggles; the reader wants to see pieces of herself. So, there are female protagonists who are popular because they don't take their heroes' arrogance lying down; they start out wanting equality and a big part of their conflict—as they tame their men—is to get it. And then there's the girl who's living her life quietly and well in a small town, who's looking for her Prince Charming, only to find that he's lived next door all along.

I could go on. But the nub of it is, the most successful authors paint for female readers a portrait of themselves as they would wish to be, gaining love and empowerment in what is still a man's world by female means and on female terms, which means a whole lot of loving, in all senses of the word!

Here are five musts for writing a heroine who resonates:

- **She's accessible**. So there is a touch of Everywoman about her. She's not perfect, and has a few flaws that she either knows about or gets to work on in the course of the story. She remains true to herself and her set of values.

- **She's sympathetic**. She bares her emotions and vulnerabilities to the reader, sharing her ups and downs, and hopes and fears. At times, this means she can be raw, even frightened. But she also has inner strength—the capacity to pick herself up, brush herself down, and keep going. She's a thinker and a doer—but she's not a whiner.

- **She's loving**. This can manifest itself in all sorts of ways, whether she battles to keep the jobs of the employees of her company, or goes against the odds for the children in her care, or is a great best friend and daughter. Because it's this capacity for love and nurture that attracts the hero to her and helps build their special world.

- **She's a traveler**. In the course of the romance, she goes on a personal journey. She may have an inner conflict that's holding her back, or find that she has to adjust or compromise on her dreams. But she knows how to give and take to be with the man she loves. And she grows.

- **She finds contentment**—as this is essentially what a happy ending is. A good heroine will start out with the resources that tell the reader she can be okay with whatever she's got, but the love of a worthy man is what completes her and brings her satisfaction.

And how to bring all of this together in one woman? Be her! Know her shoe size and what she likes for breakfast. Know her backstory and where she's headed. Climb into her skin and see the world through her eyes. Genuine emotion is what she feels and what your reader wants!

Crafting The Great Alpha Hero

by Jane Porter

In the dog or wolf world, the Alpha dog is the top dog, the leader. The Alpha male is the same.

#1 The Alpha Male is Top Dog

Film connection—Tarzan

The Alpha male isn't just smart: he's smarter. He isn't just strong: he's a prime example of male power and strength. He's usually bigger than most men, more focused, more driven, more self-sufficient.

The Alpha hero is:

- A man apart.

- A man above.

- A man alone.

In many cases, the supreme Alpha male is above regular laws. He doesn't conform, and he doesn't worry about being accepted. Public opinion is of no consequence. He has his own internal code of ethics, and he lives by it. He will nearly always choose justice—even if it's revenge.

The Alpha Hero's Strength

An Alpha hero's strength comes from his value system. His attitude and actions drive him—and he in turn changes the world around him.

In literature and film, great Alpha heroes are men who have been raised outside polite society. They are also men who have been shaped by external conflict and crisis. Think of Tarzan and Hawkeye from *Last of the Mohicans*. Both men have been raised apart from Western culture and have a strong sense of justice, and a very personal moral compass.

An Alpha's Power

An Alpha's power and strength is revealed in a crisis. He is his most dynamic when confronted by conflict. The external world must bear down hard on your hero and your hero must answer this pressure with determination and fierce resistance.

The hero might bend, the hero might momentarily fall, but the hero does not break.

It's important to remember that the great Alpha hero shines in a crisis. He is commanding. He is convincing. He is at his best—and generally the dark moment is the hero's defining moment.

#2 The Alpha Hero Doesn't Run From a Fight

Film connection—High Noon

Why does a hero return to a fight? *He has to*.

Gary Cooper's character says virtually the same thing in a key scene from *High Noon*. His new bride asks him, "Why do you have to go back (to fight)?" And he says, "I can't explain. I just have to."

It's instinctive for men to fight. They have six times the testosterone of women, and the more testosterone a man has, the more physical and aggressive he tends to be.

A heroic man cannot walk away from a woman in distress, a child in danger, or an innocent person caught in the middle of a feud.

Courage is key to the Alpha hero. Courage and pride.

As a writer creating a great Alpha hero, you cannot ever let your hero walk away from a conflict—or if you do, it must be under great distress. It must be like poison to him. It will eat him alive until he can avenge himself.

Things to remember about men:

- They're territorial.

- They are extremely concerned about providing for their family.

- They are never satisfied with a loss.

Great Heroes Have Weaknesses

Every great Alpha hero has a great flaw. Know your hero's flaw, and work it. The heroic flaw is the hero's Achilles Heel.

> *"That which makes him great, makes him weak."*

or

> *"That which makes him great, will bring him down."*

This flaw is key to plot and the dark moment. The hero's transformation is essential to the book's rising action, dark moment, and resolution. This is why your hero is at his best not in the resolution, but in the dark moment. In the dark moment, in the crisis, the hero is revealed for all his glory— flaws and all.

What are some of these flaws?

- Pride

- Stubbornness

- Inability to compromise or yield

- Inability to let others help, or sacrifice themselves for him
- Difficulty in accepting love
- Difficulty in expressing emotions

#3: The Alpha Hero's Emotional Appeal

Film connection—Last of the Mohicans

The Alpha hero taps women's secret fantasies, including the desire to be:

- Protected.
- Cherished.
- Respected.
- Unconditionally loved: physically, emotionally and intellectually.

But the Alpha hero also appeals on another level. He is the beast in need of saving, the fierce warrior in need of a haven, the tireless leader in need of tenderness.

The hero cannot find or give himself the acceptance he unconsciously craves. This is where the heroine is essential. The heroine saves, and often redeems, the hero, taming the beast, or providing comfort for the rootless soldier.

And remember, just as the great Alpha hero cannot walk away from a conflict, he does not walk away from a woman when things get messy. He may need space, he might need time to think, but he doesn't abandon her—*ever*.

#4 The Alpha hero is a sophisticated lover

Film connection—Any James Bond movie!

The Alpha hero is not a crass animal of a man. The Alpha is a man of great intelligence, and often great wit. He can be charming, amusing, and would have a sophisticated sense of humor.

He isn't always the raw, fierce beast or wounded hero. He

can be an urbane, sophisticated hero, a hero like 007 who loves fine food, fine wine, and fine women.

But let me add here, just as the sexy bimbo is never James Bond's match, the Alpha hero never settles for less than a great heroine.

In terms of lovemaking, this man knows his stuff.

He doesn't make love by the book. He doesn't follow any rules. He isn't just physical and sexual, but sensual—at least the right woman makes him sensual.

Basics For Writing A Love Scene With An Alpha Male

- Chemistry.

- More chemistry.

- And even more chemistry.

The heroine can't be oblivious to an Alpha male—not at the beginning, not at the first meet, not ever. Think about it, an Alpha male—an Alpha wolf—would demand to be noticed. He'd demand, or at least expect, attention, respect, submission.

The suggestion of submission can and should make your heroine revolt. The Alpha's strong personality is definitely a source of conflict at times. It doesn't matter if your heroine is strong-willed, innocent, or sophisticated, she still must be aware of the Alpha male and needs to feel his influence.

Remember:

- The man makes waves.

- The man charges his environment.

- The man is a force-field and he's going to impact the heroine's life whether she likes it or not, and this should create additional conflict within her. How is she going to react to such a powerful man? Does she feel anger? Fear? Irritation? Impatience? Curiosity?

This all has to come into play before the first kiss, before the first touch, before the first lovemaking scene.

#5 Love Redeems And Transforms The Alpha Hero

Film connection—The Gladiator

The Alpha hero is the ultimate in physical strength, pride, and defender of the pack. The Alpha male's position is to lead and protect, which is why this man works so well in commercial fiction.

The Alpha hero is traditionally:

- the bodyguard

- the undercover cop

- the fireman

- the police detective

- the CIA operative

- the hardened cowboy

- the scarred soldier

- the skilled warrior

He has seen it all, heard it all, been through it all. He's tough on the outside, jaded, maybe even bitter. Because he leads, because people depend on him, because he understands the realities of life and the vulnerabilities of women and children, he has hardened himself to the point of numbness. While others may not be aware of it, the Alpha male knows he will protect and defend no matter the cost.

Even if it means sacrificing himself. In fact, it's understood that he can and could die any day, at any time.

This knowledge makes him a mass of contradictions. He will love, but he will try hard to control his emotions, as well as the expression of love—and yet when he lets down his boundary, and that carefully constructed wall around his heart, he loves deeply. He is best able to show his love through actions, which is why making love is essential for this hero. It is through touch, through physical contact, that he feels closest to his mate.

#6 An Alpha Male Needs an Alpha Female

Film connection—Last of the Mohicans

An Alpha male will go to the ends of the earth for the right woman.

The Alpha might bed a bimbo, but he'll never fall in love with a weak or helpless woman. All kinds of women will be drawn to the Alpha male, but the only woman an Alpha male will choose for his mate, will be an Alpha female.

Why? The Alpha male is a leader, and he needs a lead female, or a female with the capacity to become the female leader to balance his strengths, and raise his 'pups.'

Like the Alpha hero, the heroine must be extraordinary. She is intelligent, with unusual strength of character, depth of emotion, and personal conviction. She must be able to face obstacles with courage, and handle opposition without disintegrating. At heart she is fierce, loyal, proud—and hopefully sensual, since the Alpha male is a man in his prime, she, too should be a female in her prime.

Five Resources for Research and Inspiration

I've written over thirty contemporary category romances for Harlequin and Montana Born Books. These romance are all short—65,000 words or less, but each one is still a big story packed into a tighter word count.

Because each new story needs a rich, interesting, layered world, I'm always looking for story ideas, plot twists, character arcs, and inspiration.

Some of my best research and freshest ideas have come from magazines. I use different sources for heroes, heroines, and settings.

My five favorite places to go for 'researching' my next hero:

- **People Magazine,** especially the annual issue of "Sexiest Men". I got my first sale with Harlequin Presents and have made a name for myself writing classic Alpha heroes, particularly my lovely foreign heroes. People Magazine features gorgeous men, all the time, but I'm always quick to check out People's Sexiest Men issue for new faces and new profiles such as "Hottest Import from Chile"... "Sexiest Internet Mogul"... "Sexiest Philanthropist," and so on.

- **The Wall Street Journal**, particularly Friday's Weekend section. My first Harlequin Presents, *The Italian Groom*, featured an Italian vintner living in Napa Valley. The Wall Street Journal not only gave me my information on the Northern California grape industry, but it also introduced me to a grape blight, the Napa social scene, and a small winery's expected profit margin.

  My fourth Presents, *In Dante's Debt*, (an Argentine hero and a Kentucky horse breeder) was sparked by a Wall Street Journal article on how American-bred Arabians are not considered "true" Arabians despite perfect pedigrees. Truly, the Journal is a wealth of information. Read it regularly and clip the articles that seem like they could be useful later. I have used virtually every article I have ever 'saved'.

- **Sports Illustrated.** I swear by the in-depth athlete profiles featured at the back of each Sports Illustrated issue. The articles are beautifully written, moving, and insightful. I've learned a lot about tough men, loving men, and broken men. These guys, nearly all Alpha males, dream big. They're not perfect but oh, how they try.

- **Professional Rodeo Cowboys Association website** and the **Professional Bull Riders Association.** Don't know the PRCA or PBR? Then you probably don't write "cowboy" romances, but the PRCA and PBR websites introduced me to real-life cowboys, bronc riders, and bull-riders. It taught me how the titles are won, the importance of the different events, the constant change in standings, not to mention the big events in Las Vegas.

- **All men's lifestyle magazines: GQ, Maxim, Men's Health.** I leaf through men's fashion and lifestyle magazines whenever I find a copy in a doctor's office or at a friend's house. The articles, profiles, fashion tips, travel tips, lifestyle insights are all useful. Sometimes the information inspires a character, or a career, or just help round out character details.

Sexual Tension

By Tessa Shapcott

We editors talk a lot about sexual tension. It's the lifeblood of a romance novel; without it, the central relationship just won't sparkle. But what *exactly* is it?

In a nutshell, sexual tension in a romance novel is literary frustration! Well, that is, a kind of delicious frustration for the reader, as she sees it mounting in the central relationship. But trying to generate this in a story shouldn't be frustrating for the writer; you can make it happen!

Sexual tension is the manifestation of what the hero and the heroine feel for one other; their worlds collide, their emotional intimacy deepens and their physical desire for one another increases. They are seriously attracted—*but unable to act upon it fully*.

It's also the tool with which the romance writer brings excitement and intensity to her book. It draws in the reader, whets her appetite, and keeps her glued with a mounting sense of anticipation. Good sexual tension builds in the course of the story and culminates either in an explosive love scene or a tender declaration of love.

If you're wanting to build good sexual tension, keep three words in mind as you develop your characters and have them act out the storyline:

- *Chemistry*: there has to be a potent attraction between

your main characters, which bubbles away to boiling point, until it spills over and they make or express love. They can show this attraction to one another, and thus to the reader, in all sorts of ways—through dialogue and sparky banter, through signals, such as glances and body language, or directly through actions, such as touch or foreplay.

- *Anticipation*: each character is aware of overwhelming attraction to the other, and so his and her inner thoughts and insights have important parts to play. It may be a case of trying to resist feelings, or a quiet moment of delicious sensual reflection as one appreciates the physical beauty of the other; of wondering what will happen when they're alone together, or a determination to seduce. Whatever, if your hero and heroine have a sense of growing excitement, your readers will too.

- *Teasing*: sexual tension can be developed and manipulated to build gripping climaxes and semi-climaxes. Look at varying the pace of its development; it can mount at roller-coaster speed, or tantalize as a slow burn. Think about using stop-start techniques—interruptions are always useful—and how you can make the protagonists wait. And study the power of your characters to control the pace. Who is the pursuer, or seducer? Who is the one accepting or resisting? Try teasing your audience a little with various speeds and motivations.

It's always worthwhile considering where the sexual tension between your hero and heroine is actually coming from. Obviously, physical attraction is a main driver. They fancy the pants off one another! Theirs is a desire that, ultimately, will not be contained.

But don't forget that emotional intensity as the main characters clash, withdraw, find accord, and come together is also crucial. The key to this is a strong conflict within the central relationship. Conflict is what keeps the hero and heroine apart and so makes their physical craving stronger.

It adds drama and heightens feelings, creating an emotional vortex at the romance's core.

Lastly, do enjoy it! It goes without saying that if you labor to build the sexual tension in your novel, it will feel *labored.* So here's my final tip: we mentioned climaxes when we talked about teasing—we were, of course, thinking narrative climaxes. But if your mind strayed to the more naughty kind, that's good too. Because building sexual tension in a novel can be compared to how we ladies feel when we're making love: a journey of wanting and yearning, of exploring and reaching, of receiving and letting go, in order to reach that peak of desire... are you ready?

Writing Hot: Sex, Sexual Tensions and Love Scenes

by Jane Porter

Romance novels with heat, and explicit love scenes or sizzling sexual tension, sell well in today's market. But many writers new to romance don't understand the difference between a romance novel and erotica, so let's define both right now:

A Romance novel:

- inspires feelings of love and affection.

- may or may not include acts of sex in various degrees—sweet, scorching, spiritual.

An Erotica novel:

- inspires feelings of love through the act of sex—vanilla sex, exploratory sex, and serious kinky sex.

- is not porn because it involves feelings of love 'through' sex.

To write either type of novel well, you must:

- Be comfortable writing about sex. You can't write with emotion or create believable, sensual love scenes if you are uncomfortable writing about explicit love-making.

- Trust yourself as a writer. Writing is challenging. Writing great love scenes even more challenging.

- Approach love scenes the way you'd approach any other scene in your book. You have to be confident and take risks and put it all out there, using your voice to make a love scene fresh or interesting.

Everyone knows what the body parts are and what they do, so your job as the writer is to make the scenes important to the story. Love scenes shouldn't be filler and they shouldn't be there just to titillate the reader. Love scenes should serve a purpose and move the story forward.

Arousal begins with the brain. Our minds are our sexiest organs. So engage the mind, make the reader experience the emotions, the nervousness, the adrenaline, and all the excitement. As a writer you're seducing, not just a character, but the reader too.

Great writing is about showing, not telling, and this is even more important in love scenes. In the old days, scenes ended with a chaste kiss, or the closing of a bedroom door. Today's readers expect heat in their love scenes... or at the very least, if you write sweet romances, sizzle and tension.

In today's contemporary romance, it's not enough to write that the hero kisses the heroine, or touches her. What readers today want are the emotional and physical response... How does the kiss make the heroine feel? How does she respond to him? Romance readers crave emotion and sensation, and delight in the roller coaster ride of a new relationship: falling in love, being aroused, feeling desire. The readers want to be on the ride with the heroine, experiencing the excitement, the anticipation, shyness, and anxiety that accompanies the unknown.

Speaking of kisses, that first kiss between the hero and heroine is huge. The first kiss needs to capture the essence of the hero and heroine's relationship. A kiss is more than lips touching, a kiss is about creating feelings that will develop the relationship, heighten story tension, and drive the plot forward.

Engage the senses. We have five senses. Your scene shouldn't just be about who's doing what to whom. It should be about more—the sounds, the tastes, the smells, and so on. Keep the words flowing by mentioning the things your hero or heroine would notice in that particular moment, but a love scene isn't where the heroine or hero should be thinking about bills and laundry. Keep the scene focused on what's important.

Getting Physical

Readers today expect to get a lot more than kissing in a romance novel, and today's bestselling erotica is definitely hot, sexy, and explicit. In a romance, love scenes don't usually take places until the relationship is established, or there is an emotional connection present.

In an erotic novel, sex can happen a lot more quickly. Readers expect heat, and love scenes, fairly early on. In erotica, sex can also wrap up quickly, too, whereas in a romance novel, the sex scenes are handled as love scenes, and have a slower, bigger buildup, and a more significant cool down than you'd see in erotica. Why? The emotions are front and center in a romance, and since a romance is about falling in love, the reader needs to experience the sensation of falling in love too.

In a romance novel, the emotional connection between the hero and heroine is more important than what's actually happening physically. Ground each love scene. Build the scene so the physical interaction is believable and not awkward, or uncomfortable. Seduction happens in stages. Think about the sequence of events when a new relationship is developing. There are rules for behavior, and men and women both know it. You'd never kiss before there'd been a touch to a shoulder, a hand to a back or waist, or the holding of hands.

Characters wouldn't get naked without kissing first.

Things to think about for your love scenes:

- first touch
- first kiss

- subsequent kisses
- hands and touch—above the waist
- hands and touch—below the waist
- varies stages of dress and undress
- mouth to body
- body and body
- protection (in this day and age, you can't forget to make a brief mention at the appropriate time or establish it before, or after, the actual act of sex)
- intercourse
- orgasm
- afterglow

The reader wants to know what the hero is experiencing as well, so consider your points of view, as well as what happens after sex. How do your characters feel when it's over? Do they talk, kiss, cuddle, fall asleep, or dress quickly to get out of there? The love scene isn't over with an orgasm. The scene is over when you've reached an emotional climax, whatever that will be.

And remember that the sequel to a love scene can reveal more about your story and characters than the act of sex itself.

Other Tips

- Don't use purple prose. Avoid using euphemisms or words that make you uncomfortable. Test your word choices by reading the scene out loud. If you cringe or laugh, you might need to rethink your word choices.

- Deliver on your promise. If you're positioning your story as a sweet romance, keep it sweet, don't write graphic love scenes with crude names for parts of the body. If you're writing hot, then you need to deliver heat, sexual tension, and exciting love scenes.

- Create an intense physical awareness between the hero and heroine from the beginning and build the relationship from there. Don't get the hero and heroine in bed, or naked, until they're both seriously hot and bothered. Make the reader want more. Make the characters desperate for satisfaction. Make 'em hungry.

- You don't just tease your characters with heat and tension, you're teasing the reader too. Hook your reader. Keep her turning pages, wanting to know what's going to happen next. Use all your best pacing techniques to create tension, build suspense, and make the reader wonder if these two lovers will ever come together.

- Love and lust defy reason, so create believable characters that should *not* be together, motivate them properly so the reader is invested in the conflict, and then flame the chemistry so your hero and heroine are burning up with need, and you've got a hot love scene and a reader who can't put your book down.

- Make characters real and interesting. A fully developed character is far more emotionally and sexually appealing than a cardboard caricature.

- Don't force your characters to do something just because it's what you want them to do for the sake of the plot. Romances and erotica are character-driven stories. The plot shouldn't be pushing the characters around. The characters' emotions and connections influence the story and pacing.

- Write scenes that appeal to the senses.

- Match the emotional rise in a story or scene with a rise in physical action. Or, go against the grain for erotic adventures. Why do erotic games work? They're all about mystery, excitement, adventure, and the unknown... things people crave.

- Erotica is an escape from the ordinary. It's an adventure and an experience.

- Even the hardest, toughest character can be leveled by the right touch, from the right lover. Strong men can be brought to their knees by desire and physical hunger. Emotionally frozen women, or untouchable sophisticated women can be influence, shaped, or even confused, by pleasure.

Passion On The Page

Writing Exercises to Help Add Heat and Sexual Tension

By Katherine Garbera

Sexual tension doesn't start the page before you write a sex scene. It starts on the first page of your book. Each of your scenes should be layered with all five of the senses, emotion, and an awareness of the other characters.

Even if you plan to leave the bedroom door closed, you can write one hot book. Some of my favorite books are written with so much tension you can't help but be turned on even without the titillation of BDSM or some sort of erotica.

My exercises are going to be aimed at helping you go through your own work and add in those layers that will make your book more sexy. Not by adding in things that make you uncomfortable—though as Linda Howard once said, if you're not squirming in your chair, neither is your reader—but by playing up your characters' own sexual awareness in themselves and in others.

I know it's a cliché to say that men are always thinking about sex, but in my experience it's true about ninety percent of the time. But that doesn't mean your hero has to be a horn dog. It just means that passion starts from the first moment you envision your character.

Part 1: Creating Your Character's Sex Profile

I go online to all the different magazine websites that I know have articles about sex in them when I'm creating my characters and I start to build what I think of as their sex profile. For a recent release *Sizzle* (Harlequin Blaze), I was inspired by watching *X-Men First Class* and a sort of secondary character called Gambit. He was a Louisiana gambler with a thick sexy accent and bad-boy attitude. I knew I wanted to use that in my own Southern hero Remy Cruzel. Starting with a picture of your hero is a good place to start. But if you just have a photo or an image in your head it's shallow and one dimensional. You have to fill him out and build him.

For Remy I knew that he'd be confident of himself in every corner of his life. He's a chef from a long line of famous chefs so he was raised to believe he'd be good at cooking. I wanted his food to be spicy and hot like the story I was writing. Because it's fiction and I needed a conflict, I built that into Remy as I was creating him. He's going to have some doubt underneath that confident façade—not sexually, but in his career. Has he gotten where he is based solely on his last name? This leads directly into my main story conflict... Remy is lying about who is and can't tell anyone the truth, including the heroine.

But back to the sexual tension... from the first moment that Staci and Remy meet, they feel a spark of attraction. This is one of the cornerstones of romance. Not just in the books we write but in movies and televisions shows. Even storylines that aren't inherently romances still have this because it's something intrinsic to being human. We are, all of us, automatically sizing up every person we meet and unconsciously weighing them for their attractiveness to us.

One of my favorite books is called *Intimate Behaviour* by Desmond Morris. He's a zoologist and it's his take on human intimacy. In it he compares a lot of the mating rituals between humans to animals. So some of the things we do are just gut instinct. We have no control over it. Kind of like men looking at a pretty woman as she walks by or women staring at out the window at a hot guy. Our DNA wants us to procreate and continue the species.

On the pages of our books we explore that to create that moment when two people meet, are attracted to each other, and know that it's the worst possible time to be attracted to each other. It has to be the worst time—that's how we build conflict. Even in stories where there is forced intimacy (marriage of convenience, woman in jeopardy, and so on). They find themselves uncomfortably attracted to one another because the terms of their forced intimacy mean they shouldn't be finding love now or with this person.

Your Hero

So the first question you need to ask yourself is *what kind of hero are you writing?*

- Is he aggressive in life and in bed? The kind of man who sees what he wants and takes it?

- Is he more of a charmer, wooing and seducing with silky words and smooth actions?

- Is he more reserved, hiding his desires behind a cool exterior?

- Is he serious or playful?

Your Heroine

- Is she a wildly sexual?

- Is she playful and cute?

- Is she reserved?

Assignment

Create your hero and heroine using traits that you find sexy. Use a picture to inspire you and then create the character's sexual profile and romantic backstory. No more than five hundred words.

Part 2: Getting Intimate

Now that you have sexy characters and you're ready to write your story, you need to think about a couple of other things. The way we make love is extremely intimate and every person views it in a different way. What I think makes a perfect kiss might not be what you think is one. So you have to decide how your characters feel about kissing, touching, being naked, and making love. These are all elements that make your characters and add to who they are.

First think of how they kiss. Do they kiss with their eyes open? Closed? Is it a just a brush of lips or is it full frontal contact? These are all things that make a huge difference. And is their behind-closed-doors personality different from their outer persona?

The way you describe a kiss has to have at its core a lot of logistics. Someone's head moves one way and the lips meet, there is breath, tongues, teeth, and it all has to be described.

Think about all of the senses as you describe the kiss, not just the obvious one of touch. You have to use all five of them and blend it together with the emotion of the moment. So you want to remember what they smell like — not gross smells but the scent of their breath. Were they just eating? Did he have a mint? Have you ever kissed someone and had it taste so good you had to have one more kiss? That's what you are trying to capture in this moment of that first kiss.

We kiss a lot of people in our lifetime. Parents, relatives, friends, lovers. Some of them are awkward and formal. Some are air kisses in which our mouths never touch, but in this case we need to hear about all the details of that lover's embrace. And the first time it should be noted on the ways that it is different or special. A kiss only these two people could share.

Assignment: Describe the first kiss.

Tip: I use photographs to get an idea of how kisses look from the outside and have a lot of coffee table books that are just of couples embracing and kissing. You can also think about your first kiss with your mate. What did it feel like? Remember to take into consideration physical differences like height.

Gather photographs from magazines of ads, models, real life couples kissing. Study the photographs and compare the different styles. You'll see quite a range in kissing and embracing:

- He has hands in her hair and she's holding him tightly

- They both have their eyes closed, and their mouths are pressed passionately together

- They might be looking at each other

- Their mouths might be open, as if exchanging breath.

- Is it a playful kiss? A joyful kiss?

After kissing we need to know how they make love. Is it raw and untamed? Is it soft and romancy? However they do it, you need to make sure you are capturing the emotion of the moment as well as turning both yourself and your reader on.

Think about how your characters might make love. Add this to your sexual profile. Another thing to keep in mind is if your character is different now. So let's say your hero is usually a wham, bam, thank you ma'am lover but with the heroine he wants to take his time. For once it's not about getting off but about being with her. You layer that into the way he makes love to her and his internal monologue so that the reader knows this time it's different.

Same with your heroine. Let's say normally she's missionary style lights off but with the hero she feels more confident, more emboldened and this time she's not going to be shy or scared. She's bolder, yet she still has some of that shyness and his reaction will set the tone of the love-making and also help the heroine to grow.

Assignment

Describe how your hero makes love to your heroine and vice versa. How is this different from every other time they've made love? What is the emotional punch you are going for in the love scenes? I make sure you can't skip my love scenes. I embed them with important pivotal moments in character growth.

Think about the different ways we make love. Sometimes it's gentle, other times it's raw. What are the emotions they are feeling, and how are the expressed in the moment? Set an image of the scene in your head and in the reader's mind. For example... he's fully dressed, shirt opened, and she's topless and her skirt is hiked up. This is very sexual and highly charged—so make sure that whatever is going on emotionally matches it.

Or she's more of the aggressor. On top of him and keeping him under her. Does she have the control? Or is he just letting her think she has it? How does this make each of them feel?

Or he's the aggressor, pulling her to him keeping her place with his arm around her. Is this a pseudo bondage scene where he has told her to keep her hands in place?

Part 3: After Physical Intimacy

Once your heroine and hero have been intimate you have to ramp up the sexual tension. In a romance this is when the emotional conflict is really coming into play. They are starting to fall in love and having some doubts (because of your conflict) about whether it can work. They have let this person see them at their most intimate and now they have to face them in a situation that is going to put them at odds with each other.

Each glance or touch at this point is doubly powerful. The physical intimacy has made them a pair-bond, so as soon as they touch it sends a reaction through both of them. But they are in conflict, so they have to resist those urges and try to figure out if they are going to take a risk on love and with each other.

I find this one of my favorite parts of the book to write. There is so much fun in delving into the psyche and really getting dirty in these conflicting emotions. I often set my emotional conflict up in such a way as to mirror whatever it was that hurt the character the most in the past. So if she caught her ex cheating, she's going to see the hero in a situation where he is "cheating on her" so that she has decide if she believes what her eyes are telling her or what her heart is. Because of the growth over the course of the book she'll be torn. If she trusts him she might end up with a broken heart all over again. If she doesn't, she'll never love again, never trust again, because she knows she already felt that way for him and his betrayal is killing that part of her soul.

Assignment

Describe the black moment for your characters and use their sexual profile to enhance it. So if they have been playing at domination the entire time, reverse the roles so that the other one has to experience the feeling of powerlessness. If he's always the aggressor, make her the aggressor. Change it up so that the hero and heroine both have to face the fact that something has changed and only by coming together can they move forward and they both have to give up something they haven't before.

Katherine Garbera's Keys to Sexual Tension

- Forget about your family and friends reading your love scenes! Nine times out of ten they are not your target audience.

- Create sexy characters. Make your characters the type who are willing to take a walk on the wild side if that's the type of book you want to write.

- Give them good fantasies and explore them. Remember it has to be the hero or heroine's fantasy. What turns them on? Then take them to a place where they can trust each other enough to reveal it.

- Keep the characters real. Remember your hero and heroine should sound different in the love scenes. If he's doing a lot of thinking and not focusing on the job at hand, you might want to re-look at his POV.

- Layer each scene with all five senses. Sexual tension and sensuality should be on every page of your book, not just in the love scenes. Have your characters indulge or repress all their senses. What you focus on is what the reader will know is important!

- Sustain your sexual and emotional tension until the very last page of the book. Make every scene work for you by keeping the level of sexuality high. Every time a character begins to feel comfortable sexually, shake things up!

- Write at your own comfort level. Don't try to write a hot book if you don't like to read one. Also, don't write explicit scenes unless it fits with your story and storytelling voice.

Books to Read

Intimate Behavior, Desmond Morris ISBN 1-56836-163-7

Brain Sex, Anne Moir, Ph.D. and David Jessel IBSN 0-385-31183-4

The Art of Sexual Magic, Margo Anand ISBN 0-7499-1583-8

PROBLEM SOLVING

On Process

By Lilian Darcy

What is Process?

Basically, it's how we do what we do. There's a process to cooking, brain surgery, sweeping the driveway, pretty much everything, and even with fairly simple tasks (like making a cup of coffee), no two people will do it exactly alike.

When we first start writing, most of us probably don't even think about process. If the words are flowing, we don't question why. If they're not flowing, we're probably more preoccupied with story or character issues than with our methods of work.

As our writing journey continues, though, process starts to matter.

These kinds of things start to happen:

- That terrible time with our second book where we wrote ourselves into a complete mess that took twelve drafts to sort out is not an experience we ever want to go through again, thanks very much, so we start to think about how we got into that situation in the first place.

- We start to find that we're reluctant instead of excited when we sit down at the computer. Heaven forbid this shows in the actual writing.

- We *sell* (yay!) and realize that our new publisher doesn't just want one book from us, they want three, or six, or a career's worth. We have deadlines now. How are we going to meet them? How do we deal with the pressure?

Now, and for the rest of our writing careers, we'll need to pay attention to process, and I find that the longer the career and the more books we produce, the more attention our process requires.

If we don't give it this attention, we run the serious risk of burnout, missed deadlines, a drop in the quality of our work, stress on ourselves and our families, or maybe worst of all, coming to hate writing when we used to love it.

Exercise

Think about your process, and write about it in whatever form suits you. Bullet points, thoughtful journal style, structured essay, messy mix of all of these (that would be me).

Here are some of the questions you might want to consider, but it's not an exhaustive list. Use them as a starting point. It may help to also think about other forms of process in your life, such as the way you do housework or your day job, the way you studied and submitted assignments in college. There's no right or wrong in how you do this thinking and writing, or what you come up with.

(Okay, no, wait, there's one wrong—dishonesty. The worst mistake you can make when thinking about process issues is to be dishonest with yourself. Basing a whole writing plan around, say, the statement, "I like to get up at five o'clock every morning to write before the kids are awake," when in fact they're the ones dragging you out of bed at nine, is not going to help you to understand and work on your process.)

Are you a team player, do you prefer to work alone, or do you like a one-to-one partnership?

Do you like quiet when you write, or a stimulating atmosphere?

What's your most productive time of day?

Do you work steadily toward a deadline, or is there a big, panicky rush at the last minute?

What inspires your creativity? Music? Art? Gardening?

What blocks it completely? Talking about a story too soon? Other people in the house while you're working?

Where do you get your best ideas? In bed? In the shower? Talking to other writers?

What's your favorite part of the massive task called "writing a novel?" The initial idea? Deepening your sense of the characters? Creating suspenseful plot twists? Editing a draft?

Are you a plotter or do you fly into the mist?

When you hit a problem, how do you react? Keep staring at the screen? Go shopping? Go for a walk?

When you solve a problem, how does the solution usually come to you? When you're thinking about something else? When you have pen and notebook in hand?

How do you recognize a problem in the first place? Quickly? Or only when it's beating you over the head with a brick?

When are you most in love with your book? Before you start? When you type "The End?"

When do you hate it the most?

Or maybe there isn't a pattern? Or maybe you haven't written enough books yet to know?

What are your strengths? Dialogue? Plotting? Character?

What are your weaknesses?

Are you conscious of trying to enhance strengths and minimize weaknesses, or don't you think about your writing that way?

In other areas of your life, are there some tasks you can't

wait to start and others you endlessly put off? Do you ever get in trouble from either of these things? Starting to paint your bedroom before you've put drop sheets on the floor? Putting off bill-paying until you get late payment charges?

What would others say about you and the way you handle the tasks in your life?

I could go on, but that's probably plenty to get you started.

The goal of the exercise is simply to make you focus on your own process. You may learn new things, or remind yourself of things you already know but tend to forget in the heat of the moment. You may see patterns you hadn't realized were there.

Enhancing Your Process

For all of us, the more we can fine tune the engine of our process, the better we'll write, the more we'll write, and the easier it will seem.

The good news is that the exercise we did earlier already puts us much farther along the journey than we were before. Simply *understanding* our process does an enormous amount to enhance it, as long as we keep the understanding we've gained in the forefront of our minds.

Understanding our process stops us from proceeding on false assumptions:

If you decided earlier that you prefer working alone, or one-on-one, this may explain why you dread your critique group meetings, no matter how much your best writing friends gush about how great they are.

If you decided that your panic about deadlines doesn't lead to increased productivity, you'll want to set up a writing schedule that allows you to proceed steadily toward completing your manuscript.

Unfortunately, there's bad news, too. Although we can make some changes to our process, there's a large extent to which we're stuck with it. Enhancing our process is about steering our way within the current, not swimming against it.

Exercise

Look back on what you wrote earlier, possibly with a highlighter pen in hand. Identify which elements in your process you feel are strengths and which are weaknesses.

Again, there is no right or wrong, here. Be honest (I am *always* going to demand that you be honest) and write as much or as little as you want.

You may feel some elements of your process are neither a strength nor a weakness. That's fine, too.

When you're done, take a look at each cluster of elements and see if there's a stand-out amongst them—biggest weakness, greatest strength. Pay careful attention to these, because they could make or break you.

Think and write about how you can make your strengths even stronger, and how you can mitigate your weaknesses. In this part of the exercise, I can offer a few examples, but otherwise you're very much on your own.

This is one of the areas to which you should give ongoing time and attention. You may have to... in fact you should... come back to this over and over again. *Paying attention to your process* is one of the most valuable things you can do as a writer, and the longer your career the more important it is.

Examples:

You decided: "I'm very stimulated in my own creativity by the creativity of others."

Process enhancement: Make deliberate and conscious time in your schedule for this kind of input, whether it's listening to music, going to an art or craft exhibition, watching a movie. Make time afterward to write down any ideas that came from the experience.

You decided: "I work best in a quiet atmosphere, on my own, and that's tough because I have people around me all day."

Process enhancement: Find a place where you can work alone. An odd one that most people don't think of—writing in your car. Drive it to a scenic park or lookout—or if you prefer, a busy but anonymous setting such as a parking lot—and get out your laptop.

You decided: "I work best in a huge long burst of uninterrupted day and night frenzy, but this doesn't fit with my family life."

Process enhancement: Program your frenzy into the schedule well in advance. Pay for child care or arrange a barter or swap with friends, get your house super clean and organized in advance, including prepared meals, then on your pre-arranged days, check into a motel, house-sit for a friend who is away, or go to the library or a café all day and just come home to sleep.

Changing Your Process

We've talked about steering within the current of our natural process rather than swimming against it, but what happens when this just doesn't seem possible?

In a writing career, there may be big changes which will force us to change our process. Some of the most significant of these include getting married or divorced, having babies or watching adult children leave home, quitting or taking on a day job, and selling our first book or our big series or starting to write for more than one publisher.

Again, *paying attention to process* is going to help us navigate these changes with our writing intact.

Sometimes it's obvious that our process will need to change. If we go from writing one book a year with no pressure to submit, to writing four contracted books a year, each with a tight deadline and production and promo schedule, we'd be crazy to think that our day-to-day writing routine can remain the same.

Other times, the need for a change in our process is going to blindside us. An obvious example here is when we quit our day job to write full-time, and if you've been around for a while you may well have heard the warnings about this one, or experienced it yourself. Few people realize that quitting a day job in order to write can be anything other than a positive change. All that time! No work pressure! No more squeezing our writing time into a couple of feverish hours a night that we've looked forward to all day!

The reality is often very different. A silent house instead of the stimulation of work colleagues. A task that's suddenly gone from being an illicit pleasure and escape to being the main duty of the day. All that time when we *could* write, but we could also shop or have coffee with friends or answer the siren call of the huge pile of dirty laundry on the bathroom floor.

Exercise

If your life is humming along with no big changes in your recent past or looming in your future, this exercise may not be relevant to you. You could do it anyhow, on a theoretical level, choosing a change that may happen in the future. Nothing like a little advance preparation!

Think about a life change that has affected your process recently, or that is going to affect it in the near future.

Write down some of the positives and negatives that occurred with this change, or that you envisage occurring. Brainstorm the ways you can celebrate and enhance the positives, and the ways you can deal with the negatives. What do you think was the toughest thing, or what do you think it will be?

Trouble-shooting Your Process

We've already covered a number of trouble-shooting techniques in the earlier exercises. Just thinking about this stuff in the first place is a major start. But what happens if our process problems become more serious? What happens if we land ourselves with a toxic process?

As so often in life, there isn't a hard and fast line between a process that's working and one that isn't. Almost all of us struggle with our process at times, or feel envious of another writer's process that seems so much easier and healthier. Some people actively hate their own process and end up fighting it in a way that exhausts them.

Signs that your process may be toxic:

- It endangers your health. You can't write without drinking twenty Diet Cokes or twelve whiskies or eighteen cups of espresso a day. You go for a week without walking farther than desk to bed to bathroom and you're putting on weight fast.

- It endangers your career. You are always late on deadline, not by a few days or a few weeks, but by four or five months. You spend a whole week staring at your computer screen and produce a single paragraph. You submit a manuscript that you know is bad, not just writer-angst bad, but really unpublishable-bad because you just panicked and hit "Send" like a trapped animal.

- It endangers your relationships. You and your partner fight all the time about how much time and effort and money you're spending on your writing. You keep missing your kids' activities and they eat cereal for dinner—not just occasionally but every night. You yell at your mother when she doesn't understand why you can't see her eight weekends in a row because you're working.

If any of these three signals apply to you, then you need to take action, and there may not be a quick fix. Some writers need professional counselling, a life coach, or a personal trainer. You may need to sit down and strategize with the other major stakeholders in your writing and your life.

Again, being honest is important, and so is being rational and brave. If you know you're going to be seriously late on deadline, don't string your editor along with endless promises of "two weeks" that you know in your heart aren't realistic. Tell her that you have stuff happening and you're going to need six months... and then be sensible about how you use that time so that it really is six months, not nine.

Your family will also respond to greater honesty. If you're going to be at your computer the whole weekend, better to tell them that upfront so they can plan accordingly, rather than repeatedly telling them, "Another half hour."

Learn to love the "law of diminishing returns." If you can write ten pages in four hours, this *doesn't* mean you can write twenty pages in eight hours. It's probably more like twelve pages, honestly. Recognize that leaving your computer and getting some fresh air and exercise will actually mean you get more written than if you'd stayed there all day.

As I'm writing these pieces of wisdom, I'm thinking they're not enough. If your process is truly and chronically toxic, then you will need help and support and time, and you may need to try several different strategies before you find something that works. What's more, the cure may not be permanent. Certain areas may need a red flag for your whole career.

Exercise

Think honestly and carefully about likely red flag areas in your process. Right now, your process may be working fine, but have you noticed any changes in direction in recent months? You used to drink four cups of coffee to fuel your day, but now it's up to seven? You were a week late on your first book, but two months late on your fifth? When the changes are gradual and incremental, it may not be obvious that there's a problem until it's getting serious. *Pay attention to your process.*

If your process is already wreaking havoc with your well-being, write about how that feels and about any solutions you can think of.

Common areas where people get in trouble are the ones

I've outlined above, but there are others. Spending too much time, effort, and money on promoting the last book instead of writing the next one. Lying to yourself about what you need to do in order to write ("I have to be a little drunk when I'm writing or my creativity dries up").

There's no real structure to this exercise. It's journal writing, really.

In fact, much of your work on your own process can be likened to journal writing. It's self-contemplation. It's ongoing. It's free-form.

So if you haven't started thinking about process yet, now would be a good time to start.

Stumbling Blocks

by Jane Porter

Drawing a Blank: Confronting Writer's Block

I've heard successful writers proclaim they don't get writer's block because they won't allow themselves to get writer's block. Others have said that writer's block is related to motivation, or lack of it. All I know are my own painful experiences of starting a new book and eventually drawing a blank. I've learned some techniques to help me work through my own writer's block and maybe they'll work for you.

Revisit the synopsis

If you haven't written the synopsis, do it now. You'll be making needed progress on the book (you have to have a synopsis to sell) and focusing your thinking. If you've written the synopsis, read it aloud and see if you find it compelling. If not, rethink your plot and motivation.

Write a brief outline

Break the plot into brief chapter outlines, highlighting turning points, mid points, dark moments, and so on. You can easily check character motivation with key plot elements, making sure emotional and sexual tension are in line with internal and external conflict.

Do character sketches

Sometimes I draw a blank when I don't really know a character. I need to understand my characters' history to help them make the appropriate choices for this book, in this given scene. Those choices impact both dialogue and action. By going back and doing more extensive character sketches I can often recapture a missing ingredient in conflict and tension and give the story fresh momentum.

Write backstory

Writing backstory is similar to character sketches, except that I actually write scenes that could have happened in a character's life (such as the divorce of the heroine's parents). The death of a first child. The foreclosure on the family house. The humiliating science class project. Flesh these events out, allow the character to live the experience, internalize the joy or pain. Save these scenes as creative fuel for the book itself.

Brainstorm twenty scenarios

If you know your characters and you've nailed down the plot but the story still doesn't seem compelling, write up a list of "what ifs." These can be outlandish or reasonable. What if the divorce wasn't final? What if he hadn't ever forgiven her? What if there was a flood? These possibilities might inspire a new plot twist.

Tally up pluses and minuses

If you've tried everything and the book still isn't working, re-examine why you started this book. Make two columns, positive and negative. What are the strengths of this story? What are the weaknesses? What do you like? Dislike? Are you bored with it or just fatigued? Use the list to make a decision about the book. Should you forge ahead or set it aside and start something new?

Write longhand or change your environment

If just turning on your computer makes you ill, don't do it. Take a pad of paper and a pen and go somewhere else. Write your scenes by hand. Brainstorm with a great felt-tipped pen. People-watch. Journal.

Perhaps that successful writer who said that she never allows herself to get writer's block is right. We can work through our troubling blanks with patience and perseverance. Next time you hit that wall, don't panic. Instead, savor your creativity, appreciate your gift, nurture your drive.

Sometimes writing is hard because writers are complicated people. Let yourself be complicated, cut yourself some slack, remain confident that you are a writer and the words are there, and the writing will return.

The words will return.

They always do.

Mastering Revisions

I didn't always love revision. I do now. To quote Kristin Hannah, one of my favorite writers, revision is "Re–Vision" the book. It's your chance to re-imagine the book... to take a brand new look at it and see how you can make a good story better. A great book magical.

Before Selling and Before Submitting To Your Agent or Editor

Once you're done with your first draft, it's time to do a hard edit. You've got to sit down with the book and read from start to finish.

- **Read ruthlessly**. As you read, ask yourself: What scenes don't move the story along? What passages begin to feel repetitive? What dialogue says nothing new? What love scene slows the plot down? And so on.

- **Does it hold your attention?** I know you've read the manuscript a million times, but if you, the writer, become bored during certain scenes, I can pretty well assure you that your reader is going to get bored. If you want to start hurrying over description, your reader is going to be inclined to do the same thing. Put notes on every section that seems to drag. Prepare yourself to cut hard. If you love scenes and can't bear to throw them away, edit them out and put them in a "saved scenes" folder and hang on to them for the future.

- **Make changes and read again... aloud.** After you've gone through the manuscript at least once, make all your red-lined changes. Cut out scenes and passages that bogged the story down. Now read through again, and if need be, read your prose aloud. Listen to the flow of language, the dialogue, the transitions. Does it make sense? How does it sound to your ear?

- **Trust your gut**. If you keep turning pages and it flows, go with it. But if while you're reading, you find yourself stumbling over words, fix them. Don't think no one else will stumble. They will. Never give your reader (or editor) cause to stumble. Keep the story pace brisk. Make it a true page-turner. Anticipate a reader getting sleepy—a sleepy reader puts a book down. Will the reader ever pick the book up again?

- **Be fearless.** And last, one more great quote from Kristin Hannah on editing: "Be fearless. They are just words." Don't fall in love with your language. The scenes that you adore just might be the ones an editor wants to cut out. Treat editing and revision seriously, as a vital part of the business.

Revisions After Selling

Before you've sold, when you're doing hard edits or revision, you're doing it to please your ear and eye. But once you've sold and you get revisions from your editor, it's time to sit down, focus hard, and work quickly.

- **Tackle revisions right away.** At least, read the revision letter right away and then take a day to let suggestions sink in, but don't procrastinate too long.

- **Don't panic.** No matter how long the revision letter. Stay cool. Stay positive and go through the revision letter slowly and carefully again. Highlight points, brainstorm ideas, mull over suggestions.

- **Questions? Call your editor.** If need be, call your editor a day or two after you've received revision letter and ask for clarifications. Don't wait too long. Call while the letter (and your manuscript) is fresh in her mind. Discuss the suggestions she's made if you don't understand, or assure her you do.

- **Your editor is your best friend.** Seriously. Even when you don't agree with changes, or aren't thrilled to revisit this manuscript one more time, make them. Do it with grace and confidence and zeal. I've come to view my writing as a team sport. My editor is my teammate. She honestly wants what is best for my book, understands the company's marketing plans, knows my sell-through numbers, knows what other editors and authors are doing. I am going to do everything in my power to listen to her and deliver what she's asked for.

- **Get going on the changes.** Approach them anyway you'd like—sometimes I start with the really easy things, the tiny line edits, the glitches, and then I move on to things like fleshing out scenes before I hit the really tough stuff. By that time I'm again engrossed in the manuscript and the book no longer feels cold.

- **Fatigue**. Midway through your revisions you might start feeling overwhelmed. Okay. Good. This is normal. This means you're doing some really hard writing but it's part of the process. Light some candles, put on some power tunes, call your best writing friend and tell her how much you hate writing, then make your favorite comfort beverage, and get back in your chair, at your desk, and continue.

169

- **Re-submit.** Once revisions are done, get them back to your editor pronto. If your editor knows you're a pro when it comes to revisions, submitting your new manuscript is never as terrifying because your editor knows you can fix any flaws, tighten any sagging middles, heighten any conflict, or pull out any subplot. In short, if your editor knows you can revise as well as you can write, you'll have more partials approved, more books slotted, and more positive feedback from the publisher.

- **Keep the positive attitude.** Remember—revision is a good thing. When you have the chance to revise, you're getting a wonderful opportunity to make a great story extraordinary!

Dealing with Rejection

Your manuscript has been rejected everywhere. No one is asking to see it again. No one has mentioned revising and resubmitting. So what do you do? You have a choice. You can:

- Set the manuscript aside and look at it again in a couple of months when you have some time and perspective and make a decision then.

- Solicit professional advice to see if the book has merit and then decide if you want to attempt revisions, whether it's on your own, or working with a professional freelance book editor.

- Decide that you want to publish the book yourself, just as it is now.

Regardless of what you choose, the ball is in your court. The power is yours.

I think this is important to remember. You do have power, because you never want to become a victim. Rejection can feel personal. But it's not.

Publishing is a business. Rejection is part of a selection

process as publishers choose which projects will make them money, or earn literary acclaim.

But experiencing rejection isn't easy. Having your book repeatedly rejected feels painful and frustrating and it's definitely hard on your self-esteem. I know, as I spent nearly fifteen years trying to sell my first book, and those years were very difficult on my confidence, but what kept me going was my decision to stay focused on the writing itself. My gut told me that I would eventually sell when I mastered the craft of writing, and so I dealt with years of rejection by being positive and making choices that were empowering and proactive.

Tips For Dealing With Rejection

- It's not personal. Don't make it personal. Every writer experiences rejection.

- Educate yourself on the market so you understand publishing and the current market.

- Remind yourself that publishing is a business. Yes, it takes a lot of time, blood, sweat, and tears to write a book, but it also takes a lot of time, money and energy to publish one.

- Don't submit a book that isn't ready. That's just begging for rejection.

- Manage your expectations and set small, achievable goals to help cope with the uncertainty associated with writing and publishing.

- Focus on the craft of writing and improving your craft. Be voracious about learning.

- Once your book is submitted, occupy your mind by starting a new book. Don't obsess about the book that's being shopped or in production.

- Attend writer conferences.

- Pitch to editors and agents at conferences whenever you can.

- Find good critique partners. Use them. A great critique partner can make a huge difference when it comes to getting necessary feedback.

- Read everything you can.

- Protect the writing. It's an exercise and an art form.

- Avoid judging and criticizing other writers. It just doesn't help and won't make you feel (that much) better.

- Stay positive and develop a thick skin. You'll need it once you are published!

The Upside Of Not Selling

...or at least, not selling as quickly as you'd hoped

by Trish Morey

How many of us have been there—desperately working toward getting that call, deep in the umpteenth work in progress, buoyed by a myriad of people telling us after a clutch of contest wins or finals that we're "soooooooo close" or that we're "next" and believing with all your heart that *this* manuscript will be *the one* that the editors snap up— and what happens? Somebody else sells in a two-book deal to the line you're targeting—with maybe their very first book or after they've been writing for an entire ten minutes!

Well, if it hasn't happened to you yet, don't be surprised when it does. Because, like rejections, it happens. A lot more often than we'd like.

And while you will no doubt slap a smile on your face and join in the round of public congratulations, because you are sincerely happy for them, it's also enough to make you chuck your keyboard at the wall. I mean, you've been at this for years and it's just not fair!

Well hey, I've got news for you, life's not fair.

But as hard as it is, getting rejection after rejection, if you're hanging out for that first sale contract, it's not necessarily a bad thing to take a while to sell, not necessarily a bad thing at all.

In fact there are a lot of positives for taking your time— (and hey, I should know). Here are a few.

The Apprenticeship You Must Have

Yes, we're all desperate to be published, but do you *really* want to sell that first manuscript and realize months or years later how bad it really was? Well, of course you want to sell that first book and of course it's brilliant, so that would never happen!

Believe me, we all do.

Australian author, Alison Stuart, whose journey to publication took thirteen years, had this to say:

> *"My first manuscript gained a lot of interest from publishers as well as being shortlisted for the Catherine Cookson Transworld Fiction Prize, coming second in a major contest and getting me an agent! I really believed that publication was right around the corner. I've just finished a total rewrite of that first manuscript. My toes curled when I shook the dust off it and I realised how much I have learned in the years since I first wrote The End with such confidence in immediate publication. Imagine if it had been published...!"*

You see, those years spent in what feels like the unpublished wilderness aren't wasted. Not if it helps you understand more about the craft of writing and what is good writing and what is not. Because all that time you're waiting to make that breakthrough, you're learning your craft. And if we accept that a plumber or hairdresser or heaven help us, a brain surgeon needs a few years of study and practical trials before we trust them enough to be let loose on society, what is it about writing that makes people believe they have a divine right to publication without doing the hard yards first?

And yet, it's so tempting these days to think about self-publishing a manuscript that's been rejected by a publisher on Amazon or somewhere. After all, your mum liked it, your critique partners said it was the best thing they ever read (apart from their own stuff of course!) and we all know that publishers won't take something that falls outside their guidelines, no matter how good it is, so why not self-publish, make a barrel of money, and show them what a big mistake they made?

It's so easy to think this way.

It's so easy to look at the success of a few indie authors and think you can do the same, or maybe even better.

It's so easy to push that button and upload a story and BAM! Just like that, you're published.

And let's face it, we burn to be published. So why wait? Here's the reason I think you should. You'll be a better writer if you do. Why? Because you'll be reading the books that are being published right now, reading how-to books and letting their gems work their way into your psyche, reading articles and magazine stories that will spark off a light bulb somewhere in the back of your brain for use sometime. Attending conferences and participating on supportive e-loops, and listening and studying, and all that while you're doing the best thing you can possibly do by continuing to write and practice your craft.

You'll learn how to work with editors during revisions and maybe revisions on revisions. You learn that it's not about you, but it's all about the book.

And believe me, you'll learn how to cope with rejection and develop a thick skin.

Yvonne Lindsay, a New Zealand author who also took thirteen years from putting fingers to keyboard to selling her first book to Harlequin Desire, says this of her long lead time to sale: "I think it gives you some distance and perhaps even a thicker veneer of professionalism when you do sell. You've done the yards, and you know exactly what you're capable of."

So yes, it's an apprenticeship and it's one we have to have, and as far as apprenticeships go, ours is pretty good. Admittedly the pay is rubbish, but what you do learn along the way is pure gold.

Learning About The Industry

What happens during all those years reading and writing and soaking up knowledge? You don't just improve your writing skills, you also get to know about and understand your genre and the industry that supports it. If you're writing romance, you learn the differences between category and single title and whether you really need an agent and how to get one if you do. You learn the difference between the category lines—what's so special about *Presents* and how do they differ from say, a *Desire* or *Cherish?* You learn about the different publishers and what they want. You learn about self-publishing and read the blogs and learn how this crazy business can turn on a dime and take everyone by surprise. You learn how to write a query letter and synopsis and a whiz-bang opening chapter and you have time and the contests to practice it! You learn (somewhat sadly) that writing for publication is by no means a get-rich-quick scheme except for the very few.

In fact, keep your eyes open and you can't help but learn all about this crazy publishing industry we're so keen to be part of!

Finding Your Voice

The most important weapon in a writer's arsenal—the one thing that is going to get you published more than any other—is your voice. That's yours and yours alone and for a beginning writer can be one of the hardest things to get a handle on. What are you writing? Romantic comedy? Suspense? Paranormal? Intensely passionate romance with extreme Alpha heroes and strong heroines? All of the above?

Writers, except in very rare circumstances, don't have one-size-fits-all voices (so if you ticked 'all of the above', think again!). But finding your voice—finding your niche—can take time. And writing. And rewriting. But it's worth it, because when you sell, you are going to be expected to reproduce that quality in every subsequent book you write.

You need to understand your own voice, and where it fits. It will be easier to sell, and in turn, it will be easier to brand and market yourself when you do.

And you need to write from the heart. If ever there was a formula for writing romance, that is it.

Write honestly and passionately and from the heart and your voice will sing.

The Best Friends You'll Ever Make

I may be mentioning this last, but it's by no means least. In any profession you can make friends, good friends, and sometimes even friends for life. But I've never known a profession where it is possible to meet so many wonderfully positive and upbeat people all over the world. Nowhere will you meet nicer, more generous people. Nowhere will you find a support network like that which your fellow romance writers provide.

Maxine Sullivan, who worked doggedly away for twenty years before getting the call, had this to say: "One of the best things about not selling for a long time is the wonderfully supportive friendships you make with other writers over the years—friendships that stand the test of time."

What a bonus! The longer it takes you to get published, the more conferences you attend, the more you get involved, then the more friends you'll make, and the stronger those bonds you'll forge with those going through the same struggles, experiencing the same highs and suffering the same setbacks.

Truly, the best friends you'll ever make.

The Payoff

You've practiced your craft, you've learned about the industry, and it might be five, it might be ten or fifteen, or even twenty years down the track from when you started, but when that magical call comes, you've got a big advantage over someone who sold their first manuscript within ten minutes of deciding to become a writer. Why? Because after that call it's a completely new ball game and you're going to need all the time you can get to establish your writing career, not on playing catch-up with how the industry works.

You've worked at your craft and built your confidence in your own writing abilities and you've learned what you have to do to stay published. Plus, you've built a support crew around you for the hard times—because there's no doubt you'll still need a shoulder to cry on from time to time.

It took me eleven years of writing and submitting before that wondrous first sale in June 2003. Since then I've sold thirty books to Harlequin Presents, with sales of more than five million worldwide, won two Downunder Romantic Book of the Year Awards and been nominated in 2012 for the RITA. Was that eleven-year apprenticeship a waste of time? What do you think?

So don't feel disheartened if that call is proving elusive. Don't let yourself feel bad about your writing if other writers sell before you do. And whatever you do, don't underestimate the value of that time spent while unpublished. It's not wasted—not if you use that time productively to develop your writing and voice, to learn about the industry, and to build up networks and friendships.

And then hold onto your hat, because when you do sell, you and your career are set to go straight into orbit!

EDITING, MARKETING, AND PREPARING TO PUBLISH

Importance of Copy Editing

By Rebecca Lyles

Your Great American Novel is finished and you're ready to present it to the world. You think you're ready, but is the book? Two things can make or break a book: the cover and the editing. Let's assume you have a great story. But if the cover looks as if you did it yourself and the manuscript is full of errors, no one will take it seriously. Nothing screams "Amateur!" louder than a clumsy cover and a poorly edited story.

In the olden days, books existed only on paper. A reader who found errors in a book probably skipped over them, fussed and fumed for a while, and forgot about it. Few people took the time to sit down and write a letter and mail it to the publishing company, even if they could find the address. And if they managed that, the reader probably felt better but the letter went straight into a wastebasket somewhere in New York City.

With Internet access, a reader doesn't even have to finish the book—and often doesn't—before jumping onto some website and leaving a scathing review or a rant about the mistakes they found. Ironically, these rants are often full of more errors than the book. But the point is that someone looking for fifteen seconds of fame or the opportunity to feel superior to you will find every mistake you allow to go uncorrected.

So... as an editor, I ask you, "Would you rather I found them, or shall we let the trolls find them?"

You might be tempted to say, "I don't care about those people. I just care about nice, normal readers." But those are the people who tell their friends, "I found so many errors in that book, I just couldn't finish it." They might not leave a rant on a review site, but they're not giving you good word of mouth, and they're not pre-ordering your next book either.

The Editor Is On Your Side

Editing can be an adversarial relationship (How dare she change my masterpiece?)... but the players have changed with the Internet and social media. Online reviews that are not moderated, bloggers who can say whatever they want, and some people who just like to be mean. And the conventional wisdom is that the author should never respond to them, no matter how outrageous they are. If you dignify them with a response, you only lend credibility to their claims.

So let's assume you agree that paying a professional to do a good editing job is money well spent. You might be tempted to ask, "Then why do I need to clean up the manuscript? Isn't that what I'm paying the editor for?" Yes and no. Let's look at an illustration.

Let's say you're shopping for a jacket in a specific style and a hard-to-find color. You finally find two possibilities. One fits you perfectly, but the sleeves are a bit long. You find another, less expensive, but it needs the sleeves shortened, the back nipped in, and the shoulder seams adjusted. Shortening the sleeves on jacket #1 will not affect the rest of the fit. Chances of a perfect fit are about 100%. But doing major surgery on jacket #2 might—or might not—result in a great fit. More adjustments, more chances for something to go wrong. And the cost of the alterations will make it more expensive than jacket #1.

For the cleanest final product, you want your manuscript to go to the editor as error-free as you can reasonably make it.

If your editor has two or three corrections per *sentence*, it's more likely that she'll miss something she otherwise would have caught. If it is too messy, it might require additional editing passes, and that means more cost.

Kinds of Editing

Depending on your budget and the type of publishing platform you use, you might need one editor or two. You'll most certainly need a copy editor, but you might also need a developmental editor.

Developmental editors know your genre and they look at the big picture. They might suggest scene changes, identify holes in your plot, or ask for major changes. Developmental editors give comments like these:

- "Your main character seems weak. If you want readers to identify with her or respect her, don't let her take him back so quickly—not after all he's done."

- "His transformation in Chapter Nine seems a little sudden. What happened to make him change his mind? I would insert a few scenes earlier in the book to show what happened in his life to set up this change. It just doesn't ring true."

- "The sister's appearance in Chapter Seven needs some explanation. Why haven't we heard about her before? She seems too convenient, too much like an afterthought."

- "The six-year-old talks like a little grownup. Six-year-olds don't use such mature language, and they don't process thoughts as complex as that. It's not believable. Make him sound like a child."

Developmental editing often includes recommendations on flow and plot development, and how to make characters more believable or appealing. They do not point out typos or punctuation details.

The kind of editing most people think of is copy editing and proofreading. Ideally, they are separate edits. But for the sake of economy, let's say the same person is doing both. It includes the correction of typos, misspellings, and grammatical and punctuation mistakes. But it can also include stylistic and continuity observations, such as:

- "In Chapter Two she had her hair cut in a short bob. But a week later, her hair is long, down her back, and slightly curled on the ends."

- "He was a high school senior when she was a freshman. But in Chapter Three it says he's 32 and she's 26. That's a six-year age difference."

- "He's a rough, tough cowboy. It's not likely he would say a woman had too much 'product' in her hair. Maybe he'd say 'hair spray' or something similar."

- "She wore a spaghetti-strap dress to an outdoor evening event in Chapter Four. In that part of the country, at that time of year, evening temperatures are typically in the 50s. She needs a jacket or a wrap."

This kind of editing requires both acute attention to detail and an overall sense of whether the story seems real or contrived.

Why These Mistakes Happen

Writing an entire book is not like writing an essay or a short composition. The story often spans several days, weeks, or years. It might take months or years to write it, and no one sits down to write with every detail of the story planned out in her head. Characters take on lives of their own and develop their own voices. They change throughout the development of the story, and you might even change the location or sequence of certain events. You probably don't go back to the beginning and read through the entire thing every time you make a change!

You write some parts of the book when you're full of energy and inspired. You write other parts when you're exhausted, distracted, frustrated, or just want to finish the <bleeping> thing. It's no wonder that facts get out of alignment or plot devices collide.

But the reader reads it continuously over a period of just a few hours. That's why it has to be smooth, logical, and compelling. Without toe-stubbing mistakes. Elements of the story and how they are presented need to be consistent—start to finish.

How Can You Prepare?

Remember the jacket analogy? You want to present the editor with something as close to a good fit as you can get, without requiring major alterations. Humans (including editors) are not perfect. If you have hundreds of typos, bad punctuation, misspellings, and formatting errors, it causes the editor to focus on low-level details. This low-level focus makes it more likely that the editor will miss logical or continuity mistakes that a reader might notice. So if you give editors less to clean up, you'll allow them to see more important elements rather than being overwhelmed with all the little ones.

Create A Character Description Sheet

This is the best way to keep straight in your mind (as well as the editor's) who all the players are, what they look like, and how they are related to each other. Since the information might have changed during the development of your story, be sure to go back and update it when you finish writing the book. Here's a partial example:

- Gabrielle Hunter—age 28, dark brown hair, green eyes. Tall, slender, athletic. Widow with small child. Dance instructor.

- Josh Davis—age 33, sandy brown hair, blue eyes. About 6'3", muscular build. Single. Firefighter.

- Samantha (Sam) Hunter—age four, curly light brownish-blonde hair, green eyes. Precocious, into mischief. Caroline's daughter

- Dance school is called Arabesque (note spelling)

- Restaurant is called Giovanni's Bistro (note spelling)

... and so on.

It's amazing how often authors forget (or change) the eye color or age or some detail about a character halfway through the book. And the authors created them! Editors, who did not give life to these characters, are less likely to keep all the details straight—so help them out with a reference sheet.

Check Your Clichés

Romance readers in particular tolerate, and even expect, a certain number of devices they've read many times before. One of the most common is that, in a tender gesture, the hero tucks a lock of the girl's hair behind her ear. Or, in a thoughtful moment, she tucks a lock of hair behind her own ear. In any case, there's lots of hair-tucking going on in romance novels. These devices become a problem only when you overuse them. If you find yourself using the same one too often, find another gesture or expression to add some variety.

Look It Up

Some writers like to lend an air of sophistication to a character or a scene by dropping in a phrase from another language. If you do this, make sure it is correct. In a restaurant scene, you might want to use the names of some French dishes, for example. But remember that many languages—particularly French—employ accent marks we don't use in English. So if you want your character to order crème brûlée, don't ruin it by getting the spelling or the accented vowels wrong. If it's incorrect, the character looks like a pretender rather than a sophisticate. And somewhere out there, a chef or a French teacher or some other reader who knows these things is waiting to point that out.

Use Your MS Word Features

If you use MS Word as if it were a typewriter, you're missing out on some great features that will save you time and help you produce a professional-looking manuscript. Take the time to learn about the formatting features of Word and how to use them. Make sure you understand and use all of the settings in the Paragraph section dealing with line spacing and indenting.

Set the entire manuscript to left-justified text. That means the right margin is "ragged." Although many print books use a block justification layout (both left and right margins are straight and even), the ragged right margin is easier to read—especially for editing. You can use the center justification for chapter titles.

Whether your manuscript is prepared for electronic or print publication, it has to be formatted in a certain way. If your editor and formatter have to make too many changes, there is always the chance that new errors will creep in.

The Checklist

Here is a checklist you can use when preparing your manuscript for editing:

- Make sure the Language (under File/Options) is set to the country you're publishing in. If you're publishing in the USA, set it to English (US). If it's set to English (UK), it will flag center (for centre), color (for colour), and so on.

- Use the header and footer features to insert your last name and title in the head of each page and a page number at the bottom of each page.

- Set the Autocorrect options to "curly quotes," not straight quotes. This is the form used in publishing, and it's a tiresome detail to change in a long book with lots of dialogue.

- Set the line spacing in the Paragraph tab to double for editing. Anyone who uses hard returns at the end of every line should have to pay the editor and formatter twice as much!

- Use Paragraph indent settings and alignment (left,

center)—not repeated spaces or tabs—and set text justified left.

- Check everything Spell Checker flags, but remember that a correctly spelled word can be the *wrong* word for a particular usage. Spell Checker is know guarantee that ewe don't have misspelled words. (See what I mean?)

- Indicate scene changes, passage of time, or points of view with a blank line or a line with a symbol (such as #) centered on it. Do this especially if you shift back and forth between two people who are telling the story:

   ...and that was the last anyone heard from Betsy.

   ###

   A week later, I was awakened by a knock on my door, "Betsy!" my neighbor called, "The building's on fire!"

- Check your time sequences and references. If you say something is going to happen in two days, make sure that the intervening events span two days. This is an easy one to miss.

- If you've been edited before, make a list of your most common mistakes.

- Search and Replace takes only seconds. Make several passes through your manuscript to find common sources of errors. It's easy, fast, and helps you be consistent. Do a "Find" on these items and correct any mistakes you discover:

   1. Character names.

   2. Place names.

   3. Your most common mistakes (than-then, where-were, you-your, its-it's... for example).

   4. Your clichés (for example, search for *hair* or *ear* if you use the hair-tucking one a lot).

5. Apostrophes. Make sure they indicate contractions or proper possessives – not plurals.

Summary

Whether you are self-publishing straight to ebook or submitting manuscripts to agents and publishers, a clean, professional presentation of your work is worth the extra effort. It shows that you take pride in your writing and understand the quality standards required for success. If you have written an entire book, you've poured countless hours of labor into the characters, the plot, and the emotional impact you want the story to have on the reader. When you remove the grammar, typographical, and formatting distractions, your good work shines through.

Publishing is a competitive pageant. They're playing your music and it's time to step out on that stage. Even if your book is a natural beauty, you owe it to yourself to give it the best gown, hair, makeup, and beauty-queen smile you possibly can!

Marketing 101

By Meghan Farrell

Marketing your book does not have to be a complicated process. The key is to establish goals before you tackle any marketing. You need to know what you want to accomplish when you're marketing your book.

Is your goal to sell copies? Gain visibility? Generate buzz? Secure reviews?

Once you have your goals set, you can start building your marketing plan. Some writers enjoy supporting their book and doing PR and marketing. Other writers just want to focus on starting their next novel, but either way, all writers must do some basic marketing or your novel will get lost in today's crowded, and competitive, market.

Basic Marketing Plan

Six months from publication date:

- Start developing your marketing plan

- Make sure your website is up to date, or have a web site designed.

- Have a professional and appealing headshot taken

- Book long lead print ads (if applicable)

Three months from publication date:

- Update website with all relevant publishing information like book title, pub date, and any pre-order links.

- Request a high-res JPEG of your book cover from your publisher, or your indie book cover designer

- Send clean copy-edited ms to long lead-time reviewers

- Book and confirm online ads (if applicable)

Two months from publication date:

- Approach bloggers and reviewers for book coverage, sending them a brief query that includes your high-res book cover, the back cover blurb of your story, and your social media link.

- As soon as it's available, send bloggers your clean copy-edited manuscript or galley for reviews.

One month from publication date:

- Begin social media push

- Add your book excerpt to your website

Two weeks from publication date:

- Intensify social media push

- Follow up with bloggers—secure posts, features, interviews, and contest giveaways for their sites

Launch day:

- Send newsletter to followers

- Post blog update of release

- Inform all social media pages

- Ask friends to share your news as well as post reviews

After launch:

- Update website and social media pages with positive reviews of book

Create a Budget

First, you need to decide how much money you would like to spend on advertising and promotion. This will be different for everyone depending on your circumstances. If you decide to make a budget before you start buying tons of ads and blog spots, it will save you a headache by the end of it. This way, you will have a better idea of where to allocate funds that will best fit your launch. Here are some options to think about:

Print ads, online ads, blog spots, book giveaways, contest prizes, and so on

Social Media

Let's face it. In today's world social media is important, if not necessary, for marketing. For keeping a strong online presence, social media is a must. This is also a great promotion tool because it is free. By having different social media outlets, you allow many different ways and channels for promoting your book. Our favorite sites include: Facebook, Twitter, Google+, Instagram, Pinterest.

Another way to keep a strong online presence is with your author website and author blog. It is important for readers and fans to have a way to find you online. Make sure both your website and blog are up to date and iPhone-friendly.

Reviews

Book reviews are very helpful for the promotion of your book. Sending your book off to literary journals and magazine for reviews can create great buzz for your new book. Once a great review is written about your book, you can post it as praise in the book and on the website. A review that comes from a reputable source looks great to new readers. Our favorite reviewers include: *Library Journal, RT Book Reviews, Publishers Weekly*, and Kirkus.

Blog Tour

For a blog tour, you need to develop a distribution list of influential and highly trafficked book bloggers who specialize in your genre. Contact these bloggers and see what options they have available for you. Some options might be a review post, guest post, Q&A, or just book cover post. These blogs will help to get your book noticed to new readers. I would recommend this especially for new authors. Schedule a blog tour around the release date of your book and depending on how many stops you want to do, up to a few weeks after.

Digital Publishing Checklist

- **Choose retailer (or retailers).** Where, and how, do you want to sell your book? Is there a particular retailer that specializes in your genre, or do you want the broadest possible exposure?

- **Register for ISBN**. You have to have an ISBN before doing anything with your manuscript.

- **Choose a price**. What do similar books in your genre cost? Do you want to sell lots of books? Do some research on promotions and how to attract readers with price changes.

- **Compile manuscript, front matter**. Do you have a dedication, Dear Reader, acknowledgments? At the very least you'll need a copyright page and Contents.

- **Consider back matter**. Do you have a website or blog or upcoming books? Put links to promote them in the back matter.

- **Send complete manuscript to copy editor**. A character sheet is helpful and will ensure that you get a more thorough edit.

- **Send copy edited manuscript to reviewers**. You might get a mention or a quote you can use.

- **Send manuscript to formatter for e-conversion**. Make sure all the pieces are there, and in the right order.

- **Schedule PR, marketing, blog tours, and so on**.

It's up to you how much time you want to devote to this. Try a few and see what works.

- **Follow up**. Watch the progress of your book in sales reports and keep track of any spikes that occur. What caused them? A free offer? A mention on a website? A promotional campaign? If something works, it's worth doing again later.

THE WRITING LIFE

Heroines Don't Take Potty Breaks

Six Secrets to Building the Bestselling Novel

By Megan Crane

I'm going to talk about secrets. Important secrets. Secrets that will allow us all to break through wh atever walls are holding us back and storm the publishing world, the New York Times list, that new genre we have our eye on, our dreams of hybridization and world domination, whatever it is that we want the most.

Maybe the deepest, darkest secret I can tell you is that I have no idea how to do this. No matter who I ask, they don't know how to do it either, even if they've already done all the things I'm still dreaming about so feverishly. We speculate. We hope. We ask inappropriately probing questions of our editors, our agents, our fellow writers, searching for answers. We talk intelligently about distribution and packaging and marketing and numbers and sales and all those things that sound a lot like math to me, which I've been avoiding for the better part of my life, hence my very practical decision to be a writer when I grew up.

And someone in the room—no matter what room it is, no matter where I am, no matter what year it is or what reason we believe publishing is dying at the moment—someone always seems to know exactly how we can use these things, or certain algorithms, or the ritualistic worship of particular blogs or personalities or spreadsheets or their friend's sage advice. And yet somehow they never seem to catch that same comet by the tail.

Which leaves luck, but no one likes to talk too much about luck, because those conversations too easily slip into tally sheets and points-counting and endless debates about who's getting the biggest piece of the pie. I sold my first book just over ten years ago. I've written almost forty of them so far, depending on how you count. Do shorts count? How short? 10,000 words? Online freebies? I don't know. But that's not the point. That's tallying and counting.

This is the point: *there is no pie.*

Trust me. I've looked.

I've even tried to bake my own now and again.

There's still no pie, no matter what anyone tells you. No one has a bigger piece than you. That's fear talking, and maybe a little bit of bitterness too.

The truth is there is room for all of us.

Because there has yet to be born a reader who has a set limit of good books she will read. Oh, she might make claims to the contrary, but we know better. We know—because we're all readers too—that every single reader out there wants one thing and one thing only: *that* book.

That book that keeps her awake all night when she has to get up early the next morning. That book that makes her tear up when she's reading it, or talking about it, or even just thinking about it the next day while she's supposed to be doing something else. That book that she refuses to lend out, that book she replaces or keeps extra copies of, just in case. That book she personally takes from shelves or emails as gifts to everyone she thinks ought to read it. *That* book. That's the book readers want.

So all you have to do—all I have to do—is write *that* book.

But that's actually good news, because despite how many people you know who want to be writers—including all of those people who laugh when you tell them you write romances and then claim they'd "bang one out" over a weekend if they could find the time, though not one of those people ever manages to have a free weekend for some reason, especially after you invite them to share their results with you—despite all the people trying and all the people doing it and all the people dreaming about it, there are still more readers. The world is full of readers. Which means your readers are already out there, waiting for you. All you have to do is reach them, which is easier today than it's ever been.

All we have to do is write the book. Isn't that liberating?

The real secret is that there isn't any secret. There's no magic bullet. The only thing I know for a fact works... is you with your butt in a chair, pounding out those words. There's only finishing that word, that sentence, that page, that book, and then moving on to the next no matter what happens: rejection, publication, success, hideous reviews on Goodreads, whatever. The greatest act of creation—and the secret to success—is this: sitting back down. And writing. And writing more. As often as you can.

But the magic is in the *how*, and that's what we're going to talk about. Craft.

Secret #1: You Have To Make Them Real

Romance novels are bursting with all manner of clichés, especially the stock characters. Reclusive earls. Feisty heroines. Minxes and rakes and billionaire Greek tycoons no matter the global economy. Eight lords a-leaping from the ranks of secondary characters to their own books. So many oddly Westernized sheikhs, kings and princes and assorted royals of so many made-up countries and kingdoms, that if they were all real the Mediterranean would be less a sea and more a parking lot. The laconic cowboy. The dangerous hero of vague military background who always seems to be prowling around like a great big cat in cargo pants. The spinster, the bluestocking, the party girl with a secret heart of gold. The list goes on and on. I've written almost all of these in one way or another, so believe me, that list is a list made of love.

We can all point to these clichés. We have our favorites and we have the ones we claim we'd rather die than read, until three friends who never like the same things all recommend that *one book* that does the hated thing in a new, genius way. And suddenly there you are, reading about secret babies or pregnant mistresses or werepack ménages when you swore you would never, ever sully your eyes with such nonsense again. Why? Because the author did something with those characters that made even old, jaded you *feel* them. She made them real, so you were reading the story, not fuming over *that thing* that drives you crazy.

The question isn't how can you not write these characters, because you will. We all will, because really, one reader's terrible cliché *is* another reader's genius new take on the same, and all of these stock characters are what we make of them. Can you make your characters stand out from the crowd? Can you build unique, memorable characters, and then do it over and over again with each book? Can you make these people *real*? Of course you can. But first you have to ask yourself what it is you dislike about the things you think are horrible clichés.

I tell my creative writing students to go read at least five books that feature the thing they hate the most—including one of my choosing—and then report back, and while most students decline this opportunity to test their preconceptions, the ones who do it are usually surprised by what they find.

Because all of these clichés are reader favorites *for a reason*, and once you figure out the reason, you stop thinking about what's wrong or boring or tired or annoying about the thing and start thinking about the people involved. Here's an example. I hate virgins. I've never understood the whole virgin heroine thing. I think I've written exactly one, and that was kind of glossed over, because I don't really *get it*. What's the attraction? Plowing new fields? Sowing seeds in untouched ground? How hideously patriarchal and colonial do we have to get?

But an author friend of mine who adores the whole virgin storyline and writes it often and well recently dared me to try. And I can't resist a dare. So I started thinking about it. And then I started playing around with a chapter or two, just to see what happened when this virgin character of mine was on the page. And the more I thought about her and the more I wrote, I started to *get it*.

No one who likes virgin books cares what I think about plowing metaphors or the vestiges of my feminist education. The virgin story can be about redoing an unpleasant past, with this gorgeous fantasy that it can be *that* good, *that* hot, and *that* all about you. Or it can be reaffirming your miraculous first, great experience. It's about the joy of discovery, and unlike many a tragic real life tale, virgins in romance novels are *guaranteed* a happy ending. Just like men are in real life. What's more feminist than that?

So what I learned is that my grand ideas of What I Ought To Do as a writer might be getting in my way. Readers want the story, and nothing but the story. To put it another way, readers don't care about your muse. Sad but true. Readers don't care about your tricks or your fancy wordplay or that thing in you that leads you to overanalyze every single story you encounter and vow you'll toss it all out and start *your* book anew.

Secret #2: Readers Of Romance Novels Want A Romance

Does that sound revolutionary? Because it is for me, right around page 100 of every book I write. At that point in the story, I have usually gone completely off the rails, generally because I am trying to be *very clever*. I don't see it that way while it's happening, of course. I think I'm doing whatever it is I've convinced myself I need to do. I've made it *different* this time. I've made it *special* or *intriguing*. I've taken things in an unexpected direction—and I've hit a wall.

Because I've forgotten, as I always do, that the *romance* is what matters. I'm not saying other story elements don't matter—of course they do. But nine times out of ten, when I hit that wall at page 100, it's because I've somehow neglected to focus on the romance. On the characters who make up that romance. Because if they're still complete mysteries to *me*, they're only going to baffle and irritate the reader. And the best way to make sure they're not mysterious?

Dig deeper. Go further. Know them better.

Make them real.

If we make our characters real and unique, readers don't care how many times they've read about that *type* of character before—they just want to know what happens next and how we take them on that ride to the big finish. Readers want us to make the old and the known and the familiar *feel* new. They don't necessarily want us to reinvent the wheel—unless we can do it in such a genius way that we deliver the *promise* of that wheel while simultaneously making it all new.

I'm still working on how to do that.

Writing category romance taught me—or rather *teaches* me, every day—to respect the cliché and use it like my own secret weapon, because categories are so small and Harlequin Presents in particular are so high fantasy-based that the clichés do some of my work for me, and I'll admit it. I'm lazy. I like things that do my job for me.

For example, if I tell you I'm writing about a sheikh and a virgin, you've likely read a lot of books with those character types before, or very deliberately *not* read those books before, because you hate those character types. So you've already filled in a lot of the blanks before you've even started my book. Those clichéd characters set the scene for me before I even start, because they're in your head as well as mine, like a common language.

This means that the words I use in that common language, the poetry I make from words you think you already know, is how I make those things already in your head work for me. It becomes my job to make the broad clichés come alive, and because I know you already have all those expectations, positive or negative, I can use that to power my individual characters and my story.

It's tempting to think: *Ha ha! I'm going to throw everything out and start fresh! None of those stale clichés for me!* My advice is to resist that urge, because we're not writing experimental literature here. *Tristram Shandy* wasn't a romance novel. And our readers might swoon over the odd sentence here and there, they might admire a clever turn of phrase, and ideally we can do all of that and more (because we're not machines! We're artists!) but at the end of the day? Readers want that romance.

The power of a romance lies in its emotional honesty: so take risks with emotion first. Honest, raw emotion is how a romance featuring stock characters like our sheikh and his virgin can rock readers' worlds. They're not stock characters anymore when they hurt, when they yearn, when they fight and lose and break each other's hearts, when they heal each other or battle each other's demons, when they finally face their own. In the mind of the reader who just lived that story with them? They're real.

So what makes clichés into real, whole characters?

Detail. Specifics. Sure, he's hot. But show how that hotness is particular to *him*. Not every hot guy looks the same. Feel free to spend an afternoon or ten on Pinterest to test that theory; that's what I do. My husband finds my dedication to so many shirtless photos of gloriously half-naked men suspect. I call it *research*.

Point Of View is your best tool, so don't be afraid to use it. Take us into these people's heads, as deep as you can go. The heroine might be a beautiful woman, but so what? What about her does *he* find beautiful? What about her is different, or arresting, or annoying? How does the way she frowns at him get to him and why? Why does this particular woman get under this particular man's skin—and vice versa?

Think hard about their personality quirks—What do they *do* that sets them apart? It isn't just what they say, it's how they say it. It's their gestures. Is he remarkably still? Does she talk with her hands when she's nervous? It's whether they're quick to anger or preternaturally calm. It's how they look at each other. It's what they see and how they process it.

Think about your two favorite people. How are they like each other? How are they utterly unlike each other? It's a kneejerk reaction to use physical descriptions to show readers differences on the page, but you want to find the rawness, the realness beneath that. Real people have layers and contradictions. Real people have things they never talk about, and other things they talk about too much. Armor as well as sudden transparency. Your job is show the reader what makes these people tick, what makes them real, what makes them so fascinating to each other.

Answer that, and you're on your way.

Secret #3: Love Hurts

And so should your characters. As much as possible, and this is true even if you're writing a sweet comedy.

Emotional risks—and the consequences of taking them— make impossible-to-put-down romances. And if we find we need to push our own boundaries and take our own artistic risks to get our characters there, well, all the better.

Emotional honesty really is the key to writing romance. It's how it all works, from high fantasy books to homespun, realistic stories. It's how and why readers believe you no matter where you take them. Root them in emotion and they'll follow you anywhere. But emotional honesty doesn't mean the characters are sitting around talking about their own self-actualization. Sometimes it's better if your characters are in complete denial about what's happening to them. Sometimes it's better that the emotion be so intense they're *forced* to finally face it because they have no other choice. Maybe they don't know love, they don't want love, they don't acknowledge love, they know their love is a dark thing that will ruin whoever it touches—or all of the above. We call that *layers*.

It doesn't matter *how* the emotion finds your characters, only that it does. It can be sweet and inevitable. It can be a rush. It can be erotic or chaste, shattering or joyful. It only has to be honest. A sharing of souls, a baring of true selves.

Falling in love is scary because intimacy is scary.

It's nakedness, figurative and literal, and it's what readers want from your stories, so they can experience it vicariously through your characters—all while knowing that unlike in real life, it's all going to work out.

Of course, your characters don't know it's all going to work out. They don't know they're in a romance novel—they didn't get to read that back cover blurb. And that makes all the difference in the world. Your characters don't know where they're headed.

That means that no matter how tough it is to write, they have to act from that position. It might get ugly. It might get dark. They might do bad things to each other, hurt each other. I've seen this called "the dark moment," but I think it's never really just a moment. It's that tightrope walk. That yearning they have to believe: that this is real, that this person can really love them back, that they can love at all, whatever—versus everything they've known to be true before then. Love illuminates them, changes them. Gives them hope, makes them whole. But in order to do that, in order to make it real, you have to really go into those raw places.

Think about how hard it is to tell a stranger the true and important things that make you who you are; think how difficult it can be to tell those close to you how you truly feel about something painful. It has to be at least that difficult for your characters to open up to each other, to find their way to each other. Because people who don't know that they're the hero and heroine in a romance novel hide. They pretend. They sometimes lie. The reason they (we) do that is because there are consequences for showing our true selves, for taking risks, for being completely honest. If it were easy, no one would ever claim she was fine when really, she's falling apart.

The love story is the critical, beating heart of your book. It's what the readers want more than anything, and it should *hurt*. It should scare both of the main characters. It should be as terrible as it is wonderful, or why are they so wound up about it—and more importantly, why is your reader spending two or three hundred pages with them?

So how do we push boundaries, take risks, push the envelope?

First of all, identify the monster under the bed: what are they afraid of? What's the worst thing that they can imagine happening? Who do they think they are?

Their imagined worst thing should threaten all of that directly, so that risking it is risking *everything*. The harder it is, the better it is—because the more painful it is, the sweeter the eventual happy ending. Too many writers balk at really, truly putting their characters through the ringer. One way to tell you're doing this is when you really, truly don't want to write something—is that fear talking? Are you pulling your punches? We all do it sometimes.

The truth is that hard scenes often come from hard places inside of you; it can be really painful to mine some of the dark things you have hidden away in there. You may write entire pointless books to avoid really getting into those things, but you must get there eventually. That's what revisions are for. You owe it to your characters as well as your readers: if you can't face it, how can they?

No one will ever know if you sobbed over your keyboard or if you felt sick or if you hated every second of getting that darkness on the page—but they'll know it if you don't.

They'll feel it on every page, and they probably won't finish the book. That's not what you want. You want to give your readers what *they* want.

There is no wasted emotion in a romance novel. There is no "too far." Go for it.

Make it hurt, and you make it real.

Secret #4: This Isn't Gymnastics

This is where the sex scene comes in.

Sex helps people feel closer to each other thanks to all those lovely endorphins and the romance hero's vast skills in bed, but at the end of the day, it's just sex. If it takes the place of emotional honesty between the characters—if it's just gymnastics—the reader will be let down.

Sex scenes are one of your best tools, no matter the heat level you use. Sex scenes are crucial to understanding your couple, their relationship, their hopes and fears, and how they communicate (or don't). All that and an orgasm, too, because with very few exceptions, all sex scenes in romance novels serve to foreshadow the couple's happily ever after.

They can achieve happily ever now when they have sex, which is why we believe they can do it later in life. This means they have to have the kind of sex that's emotionally revealing as much as it is physically satisfying. A kiss can accomplish this, if that's the kind of book you're writing. Fingers touching. A glance deep with knowing, with recognition, with hunger and need. It doesn't matter how your characters touch each other, so long as they do, and so long as when they do, they are naked in new ways with each other. That they *see* each other as no one else could.

I like to think of sex scenes as emotional scenes written as action sequences. It's easy to get a little lost in logistics and word choices, but the fact is: if the reader is with you, they don't care what you call it. Really, they don't. I have read a lot of books that use words that I not only would never use, but don't even like, and they only pull me out of the story when the words aren't words the *characters* would use. But if we're deep in a character's POV and he or she is using words that seem true to who they are? I don't care at all. I only care that *things are happening*.

I've heard readers say that they skip over the sex scenes. I know I've done that sometimes, but when I do, it's almost always because somehow, the sex scene is taking away from the story rather than adding to it. Sex in romance novels should *be* the story. It should be as dangerous and multi-layered, as hopeful and terrified as your characters. It should change them, or why bother? It should force them into intimacy when they're not ready, so they're forced to contend with what that does to them afterward.

Intimacy, after all, is what's happening here, no matter where they are in their emotional journey, and intimacy is hard. It should be hard. People talk a lot about how monogamy is hard or marriage is hard or life is hard. But I really do believe that intimacy is one of the hardest things there is, because it demands so much, and it never relents. There's no finish line. You can never declare yourself "intimate" and then done. Every level of intimacy you reach with someone means there's another level waiting. It's a fire that smolders but never burns out.

This can be pretty difficult in real life. In romance novels, it's everything. And sex is where characters in romance novels burn themselves with that dangerous fire, again and again.

Secret #5: There Are No Potty Breaks For A Reason

Imagine for a moment that we recorded each and every potty break our heroines took. After all those romantic dinners, those flirtatious interactions, those sizzling consummation scenes. What if we stopped and noted that she went to the bathroom?

She'd probably have to, of course, if she was real. But heroines only take potty breaks when they are discovering that they are pregnant, as far as I can tell. Every stomach flu is a baby, and every toilet trip somehow confirms it. Or confirms she's not. But aside from plot-relevant visits to the bathroom, we don't talk about when she has to go or when she does go or anything else. Why not?

Sure, it's slightly unsavory and not a fantasy element by any means. But that's not why we don't do it. But to explain what I mean, I need to tell you about candlesticks.

A while back I locked myself in my office after a very long and frazzling day of a thousand errands that had to be done *right that very minute* and settled in to get some writing done. And I did. I am nothing if not capable of forcing myself to do things I find unpleasant which, I must tell you, was certainly how I would describe sitting down to start the day's writing at 9pm.

I knew exactly what scene I wanted to write, and I attacked it with gusto. It was when I found myself describing the ornamentation of the set of candlesticks atop the fireplace mantel in unusual (and wholly unnecessary) detail that I had to stop and admit something to myself that I already knew: the scene was not working. At all.

My first clue was the fact that I'd spent paragraphs upon paragraphs waxing rhapsodic about the decor. I was writing a category romance. While details of the hero's lavish wealth are always a part of the line I write for, there are details that set the scene and help ground the emotions of the characters in the world I've made for them, and there are rhapsodic descriptions of candles neither character would ever notice in a million years, so busy are they falling in love and failing to admit that to themselves or each other.

My second and more pertinent clue was the fact that what I was writing felt like the typing equivalent of slogging through waist deep mud.

Every. Single. Word. About. The. Freaking. Candles. HURT.

I found myself online, researching the kinds of candlesticks that might be present in an eighteenth century London townhouse handed down to hereditary heirs across time.

Excellent information to have, were I writing a historical romance novel.

I wasn't.

At some point I gave up. I staggered off to bed and collapsed into it, entertaining the usual litany in my head: my career is over, I will never finish this book, I have no idea how to write books anymore, this book is harder than all the ones that came before—all of which now seemed, in my memory, to have been written in a great gleaming burst of easy and delightful creativity—

That made for restful sleep.

And then I woke up the next morning and faced the obvious: I'd started the scene in the wrong place. I had to throw out all my work (and my genius observations about candlesticks) and start over. The minute I admitted that to myself, the truth about the scene itself became clear to me. I didn't need *that* scene at all, in fact. It was a time-waster—merely going over things that I'd either already made clear or would make clear in future. Once I accepted that, ideas for the scene I *should* have been writing all along began to come fast and furious.

I learned three things from this:

- Pay attention to the candlesticks. Or whatever it is you find yourself writing on and on and on about, that has nothing at all to do with either the emotional growth of your characters or the forward momentum of your plot.

- If you hate the candlesticks while you're writing way too much about them, it's probably because you should be writing something else instead. Stop, regroup, and let go. This can be hard, particularly when you're writing feverishly to a deadline and cutting out a day's writing can throw you behind schedule. But if you can cut, you should cut. And your book will be better for it, I promise. Though you may need a lot of caffeine to get you through the sleepless nights as you race to get back on track.

- Sometimes you need the candlesticks to get you where you need to go. I don't believe that there is any wasted writing. Did I really need pages and pages of swooning observations about the decor? Well, no. But I needed to *write* those pages. I needed to head off down the wrong path for a while, so I could see the right path so clearly. Maybe I worked out the right scene in my subconscious while I was nattering on about the mantelpiece. Maybe I figured out what my characters should have been doing while they were... not doing it. But one thing I know is always true about writing books, even the bad scenes you throw away? *The only way out is through.* Sad but true.

And what do candlesticks have to do with potty breaks? Just this: it's all potty breaks, these things we do to slow ourselves down. Candlesticks are delaying tactics and potty breaks are the lies we tell ourselves to keep ourselves from the page. We wouldn't let our characters carry on about unimportant decorating choices for ten pages, and we wouldn't let our heroines keep running away from important scenes to hit the toilet. So we can't do it either. Be like your heroine. Step away from those candlesticks, concentrate on the romance, and stop pretending you have to go to the bathroom when really, we all know we're much happier when we write.

So make yourself do it. Write.

Secret #6: Happily Ever After—It's What They Need, Not What You Want

I have a problem with epilogues. This problem is simple: I can't stand them. All those happy babies, possibly twins, and all that lounging around on picnic blankets in the delirious sunshine. These things have never appealed to me as a reader.

I always like the end of the chapter before, not the coy "nine months later" epilogue where the hero is pacing around in the throes of new fatherhood while the mother smiles like a newly-minted saint or the more-like-an-anvil "many years later" one with all that fertility in such evidence on that blanket somewhere. I never write epilogues if I can help it. I pride myself on this, because this pleases my muse.

It does not, however, please my readers, as many of my reviews make clear.

And much as I like to follow my muse—even though she's proven herself completely unworthy of this faith and has had me write entire insipid books consisting of one long, pulled punch I then have to feverishly revise—I'm beginning to realize that what I think I like as a reader is actually what I think I *ought to like* as a writer.

The truth is, I was a romance reader long before I was ever a romance writer, and I need that happily ever after. I need to *know* that the people I love are okay and going to stay okay. There are long-running series that I love dearly but am afraid to read any longer because I'm terrified something will happen to the people that I need to keep imagining forever blissful.

I may not *like* the fat babies and happy couples epilogues, but I suspect I *need* them. Joss Whedon, who created *Buffy: The Vampire Slayer*, once said something to the effect that he gave fans what they needed and not what they wanted, and it's always stuck with me. Because this is precisely what we try to do in our writing, isn't it? Characters, like people, don't always need the things we wish they would. They don't always behave. Then again, neither do we.

Ask yourself: what do these characters *want*? And then find ways to make sure they don't get it, because that makes for an excellent story. Because what do they do then? What does not getting what they want do to them? To your story?

Then ask: what do these characters *need*, and how can I give *that* to them instead? Because that's where the magic is. That's the meat of it, the good stuff. Because we know that what they need the most is each other—but they don't know that. So you have the fun of showing them.

And then ask yourself: am I doing this (writing the scene in a certain way, forcing myself to write a book that feels like it's gone off the rails, banging my head against this or that wall, pulling punches and otherwise failing these characters) because I *want* to or because the story needs it? Because I find that when I ask myself that question, things get a lot a simpler. The story needs to be told. Often, I need to get out of its way. And the sooner I accept that, the sooner I write myself straight on into another happily ever after. Even if it means an epilogue.

Here are our Six Craft Secrets that will hopefully make us all bestsellers, or at least help us think about our writing a little bit differently:

- Secret #1: You Have To Make Them Real

- Secret #2: Readers Of Romance Novels Want A Romance

- Secret #3: Love Hurts

- Secret #4: This Isn't Gymnastics

- Secret #5: There Are No Potty Breaks For A Reason

- Secret #6: Happily Ever After—It's What They Need, Not What You Want

And here are six other secrets that are maybe just as important:

- No one really knows how to do this. They just do it anyway.

- There is no pie. Anyone who says otherwise is afraid.

- Your comfort zone is there to show you exactly where to push. The harder you push, the scarier it will feel, and the more honest you'll be on the page. This is your job. This is the art and terror of writing. You can't expect your characters to do things you won't.

- A pulled punch is a lost reader. Don't do it. Yes, it's hard

213

to write those raw things. If it wasn't hard, all those folks who still haven't written that book over the weekend would be bestsellers by now.

- Intimacy is always difficult. Don't let your characters get away with pretending otherwise. Don't let them off the hook. Don't let *yourself* off the hook. You really can write that book that simmers there in your head, just out of reach. You can. You just have to do it.

- Think about candlesticks and potty breaks, and write accordingly. These two things lead to happily ever afters. Failing that, they're such ridiculous things to think about that they'll make you laugh, and we can all use a little more laughter in our lives. Our characters choose joy over fear, and they always end up where they need to go. So can we. We choose the words, we write the scenes, we get to decide.

Happy writing.

How To Play Nice With Your Dragon

by Jane Porter

The Challenge of Being Creative

> *"Zest. Gusto. How rarely one hears these words used. How rarely do we see people living, or for that matter, creating by them. Yet if I were asked to name the most important items in a writer's make-up, the things that shape his material and rush him along the road to where he wants to go, I could only warn him to look to his zest, see to his gusto."*

—Ray Bradbury, *Zen in the Art of Writing*

Being a writer makes you special. There are lots of books that will tell you how special you are, how special your creative muse is. They'll try to celebrate your creativity and help you embrace it, but most of those people writing those books aren't working writers like us. They are not paying their bills with commercial fiction, nor are they on deadline, writing anywhere from one to six books a year, year after year.

For those of us who write daily, meeting deadline after deadline, being a writer isn't always lovely and special. It's closer to addictive, maddening, agonizing, exhausting.

I have a different view of the creative life. I have a complex relationship with 'the muse,' so I'm not going to encourage you to spend lots of quality time getting to know yourself, or suggesting that you take your muse on dates. That's not me. Maybe it's because my muse isn't the kind you take on dates. You see, my muse is a dragon. A really big scaly green dragon with a mammoth tail, long nose, and sharp, lethal teeth. My dragon breathes smoke and fire and if it's really upset, it can kill.

In my world, I have to learn how to write, and live, while keeping a man-eating dragon happy. I've learned the hard way what the dragon will and won't tolerate. The list is a little lengthy, so here's the short version. My dragon objects to the following:

- criticism

- negativity

- pressure

- insults

- derogatory people, insensitivity, impatience, rudeness, and so on

You see, the dragon lives inside me—and has lived inside me for virtually my whole life. I didn't understand my dragon until fifteen years ago. Most of my life I felt possessed by the muse—driven, manipulated, controlled.

I hear voices in my head, but they are the voices of characters waiting to have their stories told. My drive to create is as much a part of me as breathing. And for those of us who are creative, we've experienced a great deal of pressure and pain trying to 'fit in,' to be part of the world, when we might just not fit in and would be far happier marching to the beat of our own drum.

And actually, we would be better doing our own thing. You see, we writers aren't like everybody else. We're home to a huge, gorgeous, mythical creature—the muse—and sooner or later we've got to come to grips with the realities of living with such a beast.

It took me years to understand what the writing lifestyle— what being a writer—encompasses. And there are periods when I wish to God I didn't write, when the responsibility of living with, and sustaining such a mythical creature, can feel overwhelming. It's easy being a writer when the dragon is happy, and when I'm relaxed and warm and content, the dragon snoozes along, happy, too. But when I stress, panic, or hate the writing, the dragon gets mad and it's war. The dragon will go for my jugular every time.

So how to keep a dragon happy?

- The dragon wants pretty much primary importance in your life.

- Your dragon wants to be told he or she's beautiful.

- Dragons like regular cycles of activity and rest (your dragon has to be allowed to sleep—a lot. In fact, a sleeping dragon is a sign of a healthy life.)

I also know my dragon is happier when:

- I feed him.

- I let him play.

- I give him space

- And when he needs to fight, I don't make him act like sissy cousin Puff.

What I'm trying to say about creativity and the dragon symbolism is that for us, who choose to be commercial writers and yet remain devoted to craft, we can't afford to let our muse run the show unchecked, showing up at will, deserting at will, generally creating havoc. A dragon run amuck is not a good thing. A dragon out of control eats villagers, creates terror, spits fire—this dragon is not helping anybody and would generally be hunted down by the hardier castle knights and warriors and put to death. Not a good end to a beautiful, mythical beast.

Not what we want for our own dragon.

And that's the fine line we walk—allowing the dragon healthy independence without letting the dragon control the future.

How Do We Succeed As Writers?

Define Your Expectations

First, you're going to need to do two things to answer the question. Only you can answer the following, and I want you to take a moment now, and answer on your handout, scribble something, but later, come back to this, and really think about it. I would spend the next year of two thinking about this as well. It's not something that's a snap decision; you have to be able to live with your goals—and yourself—to be truly content.

How do you define success?

How do you define success for *yourself*?

What are your goals for yourself, short term, and long term?

You won't be content until you know what it is you're striving for. If you're like many writers, you will always feel a vague restlessness, a craving to create. But you need to learn how to separate the creative instinct from personal happiness. Put another way, the dragon will always be there, and you can be happy—fulfilled—if you put the dragon on your team, make the dragon part of your family and your world and stop trying to make the dragon fit into everyone else's world. The dragon is essentially good and shy and lovely—don't make the dragon suffer needlessly. Don't you suffer needlessly.

Stop comparing careers, lives, goals. Have your own goals, have your own definitions of happiness and success and focus on that.

Be Prepared For Pitfalls

Problems we face as (commercial) fiction writers:

- Fear of rejection.
- Fear of criticism
- Fear of failure (or just as bad, fear of publicly failing)
- Burning out
- Getting "blocked"

Problem Solving

- Understand risk. Understand the nature of creativity—it's demanding. It's full of risks. It's full of intangibles. It's not black and white, but full of gray.

  You must also understand the nature of being human—we're going to fail, and we're going to make mistakes. It's impossible not to make mistakes, especially when trying something new, or pushing ourselves to the next level.

- Anticipate problems. Everyone has fears, and everyone will struggle. We won't however, struggle over the same issues. We don't all have the same issues.

- Silence the critics. It's inevitable that someone, somewhere is going to throw a dart at you, or your work. That, unfortunately, is human nature. You can't change people, and you're not going to change human nature, so the best thing to do is be prepared. Be on the offensive.

  Just as you should anticipate problems, prepare in advance for your critics' objections. Anticipate potential criticisms, or skepticism, and if possible, have an answer for each possibility.

- Analyze and understand the process. How do you plot? How do you deal with the void—the vacuum? How do you cycle out of it?

- Unmask writer's block. The best way to deal with writer's block is to never get it. Some writers never do. Theoretically there is no reason to get it, but if it happens to you, experts generally agree that it's caused by one of these three things:

  1. Failure of will

  2. Setting standards too high

  3. Excessive need to please

  And remember, it is the process of writing and rewriting that makes fiction original and profound. One cannot judge in advance if a story or idea is good. So stop criticizing yourself while doing, and just do. It's okay to do things badly. It's okay not to get it right, right away.

  And for those veteran writers out there, we have to be extra careful to remember that just because we've written a half dozen or more books, doesn't mean writing ever gets easier. If anything, it just gets harder. We grow impatient with ourselves and our ideas. We forget how exhausting the process really is.

- Eliminate distractions. But what happens if we lose focus? What happens if you do look out to the world for validation, look to an external reward system— advances, bestseller lists, contracts—and you feel... lacking? What happens if you lose your calm?

  In *The 12 Secrets of Highly Creative Women*, Gail McMeekin, describes what she calls as "Serenity Stealers," those things that operate as negative life choices.

  What kind of trouble? Some potential pitfalls in my life:

  1. email, Internet, social media

  2. messy desk, office, or house

  3. phone calls

  4. interruptions, whether from kids, husband, friends, or fellow writers

5. stack of bills, or paperwork piled up somewhere

6. meetings, commitments, errands

Get on top of the stuff overwhelming you. Simplify. Focus. Get centered.

From Hapless Victim To Warrior Woman

We need to develop a Psychology of Power. Most of us weren't raised to think of ourselves as warriors. Most of us were raised—like most women in our society—to try to please others.

Because we were raised to please, we're vulnerable to the judgments of others. We tend to put others' perceptions and judgments above our own. We literally give away our power, deferring to others, and yet deep down, we're frustrated and angry that we've told ourselves what amounts to a lie. No one has a right, or better answer. No one knows that much more than you do. No one knows better than you what's right for you. No one can define creativity or art for you, either.

Safety In Numbers

Kate White, author of *Why Good Girls Don't Get Ahead but Gutsy Girls Do*, says that good girls have a problem going with their gut, or trusting their instinct, "because it often means going against what other people think." White adds, "What a good girl wants is consensus. When she gets consensus, it not only means that she's managed to please everybody—a high priority—but that she's guaranteed herself safety in numbers."

And yet, trusting your gut is essential for anyone in business, and particularly vital for those of us who write. People who are overwhelmed by constant analysis, lots of rules, and negative vibes, will never pursue the boldest, most creative rule-bending way of doing something.

To develop a psychology of power, to begin to think like a

warrior, you must:

- Trust yourself.

  You can't give away your power. You must trust yourself to write. And to write well, you must stop thinking—stop over analyzing—stop forcing plot, stop playing little dictator as if you're immersed in a do-or-die game of Twister—you have to let go of the writing.

  In Ray Bradbury's *Zen in the Art of Writing*, Bradbury shares that for ten years he kept a sign taped over his typewriter that read: Don't Think!

  Don't think... *do*.

  Do.

  There's something to that old Nike slogan, *Just do it*. Whether it's running or writing, it's true.

- Fight only for what you believe.

  Therefore, if you trust yourself to write, then you're only going to write what you truly believe in, write only what you're passionate about.

  To share Bradbury's formula:

  What do you want more than anything else in the world? What do you love, or what do you hate?

  Make a list of everything that fascinates you... ideas, people, places and write about those things. Focus on your passions and stay there. Don't be sidetracked by someone else's heart or dream.

- Ignore the critics.

  Sometimes in our industry, we spend huge amounts of time and energy fearing or fretting about reviews. I know I have, especially the reviews in RT or on Amazon, and yet those reviews haven't killed my career, and I've no intention of letting them control me, either.

  When faced with a crisis, change, or tons of information, Kate White said she goes into her office, closes the door, and listens to her instincts. Ask yourself, "Would I and my friends, as consumers, want to buy this?" Or, as we're writers, "Would I want to read this?"

Be honest. And there you have your answer.

• Slay the green-eyed monster or, Thou Shalt Not Covet Thy Neighbor's Dog (Dragon).

Quite frankly, your dragon is sick of being told that he or she is inferior as well. Think about it... as pet owners, we love our dog or cat. You don't look at your dog and think, wow, I wish he were like my neighbor's dog. My neighbor's dog is soooo much smarter. My neighbor's dog can shake hands and roll over and run a twenty-yard dash. My neighbor's dog has even been invited to appear on David Letterman's Stupid Pet Tricks.

No, you think, how great that neighbor's dog is, but you still love your own dog—and you love your own dog more because you feed that dog and pet that dog and that darn dog loves you. That dog would follow you anywhere and wouldn't know what to do without you. And it's the same thing for your dragon. Your dragon loves you and needs you and doesn't care about the neighbor's dragon, doesn't want to hear how great the neighbor's dragon is. Your dragon just wants your attention, and that's the only dragon you should be thinking about.

Final Thoughts on the Writing Life

Do you want to be a published author?

Do you want to succeed as an author?

I do. I want to be successful. I want readers to love my books. I want them to come back for more.

I want the career, with the challenges, and the demands.

So yes, I want it.

It's that simple.

However, that doesn't mean I don't suffer from self-doubt, get the blues, or struggle with my creative muse, because I do (*a lot*), but my desire to write, and my desire to publish, is even stronger than the fear and the sacrifices I've had to make.

But sitting down at the keyboard, finding the words, searching for a great metaphor or the next crucial scene is only half the battle of writing. As romance writers, we also have to choose to write great fiction, great *commercial* fiction, fiction that appeals to the readers and the market.

I'm not advocating writing to guidelines, but writing with an awareness of guidelines. The romance writer must write to please herself (her own worst critic) and yet find a market for her stories and her voice. If you want to publish, if you want to be part of the genre, you'll know the market and you'll constantly work at improving your voice.

I'm not a professional author, but I am a professional writer. I take writing seriously. I have regular office hours. I give myself tough deadlines. I finish books and submit them.

As a professional writer, I read my friends' manuscripts. I read friends' books in print. I read the "competition." But in the end, when I come back to my computer, I look for "me" in my stories. I look for the hooks, the motivation, the conflicts, the characterization that makes a book real for me. I can't write with anyone else's voice. I can only write as Jane Porter and that has to be good enough.

It is good enough.

Part of being a professional is choosing to think positively, learning to set goals, and focusing.

And we must write. Every day, or as often as possible.

Truly, if you want to write and publish, you will. But you have to want it badly.

For some of us publishing will be easy. For others, it will be a tremendous test of faith and will. But it can be done. I first submitted an untitled manuscript to Mills & Boon when I was eighteen and a freshman in college. I had my first sale just before I turned thirty-six. In between my first attempt and my first sale I wrote more books than I care to remember, cried more nights than I'm comfortable sharing.

I poured my heart and soul into manuscript after manuscript but I never gave up because deep down, deep inside me, I believed I could do it. I would do it. And finally, I did.

So do you want it, or not? It's all up to you.

And that is seriously good news.

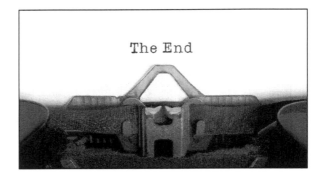

Glossary

Here are some useful terms relating to writing and the publishing industry. Most, but not all, are used in this book.

agent—A hired representative who sells your written work to publishers. Most reputable agents are paid a commission based on a percentage of the sale price of your work.

ADHD—Attention Deficit Hyperactivity Disorder.

antagonist—A villainous or troublesome character. One who causes problems for the hero or heroine.

backstory—Past events that affect or explain the current story action.

BDSM—Bondage, domination, sado-masochism. Forms of sexual activity sometimes described in erotica. Popularized by the *Fifty Shades of Grey* series.

blurb—A short paragraph or sentence about a book, sometimes printed on the back cover. Often a comment from a reader or reviewer.

byline—A few words that identify the author of a website, article, or blog. Most magazines and online publishers print the writer's byline.

character description sheet—A document some

authors provide to the copy editor as a reference for the ages, physical descriptions, and relationships of characters in a book. May also include place names or unusual spellings.

climax—The point of greatest intensity in a story. A crisis, a dilemma, or emotional peak. Also known as the "black moment."

FWIW—For what it's worth.

galleys—The first typeset form of a manuscript, sent to an author for review before the book is printed for commercial sale. Also sent to reviewers for advance promotional reviews. Galleys are also known as Advance Reading Copies, or ARCs.

HEA—Happy ever after. The desired ending for a romance novel.

hi-res—High resolution (referring to photographs). Fine quality, clear and sharp—the best kind of photo to use for your website or author biography.

hook—A literary device that engages the reader, captures the imagination, and makes the story compelling.

ISBN—International Standard Book Number. A 13-digit number that uniquely identifies a published book.

JPEG—Stands for Joint Photographic Expert Group. A popular photo format widely used in graphic arts and publishing.

markets—All the publications or publishing houses that buy manuscripts of articles or books. *Writer's Digest* publishes a yearly updated version of the *Writer's Market*, listing all the different publishers and types of materials they buy.

ms—Abbreviation for manuscript. Plural is mss.

muse—from Greek mythology, the source of inspiration for literature, science and the arts.

novel—A fictional work, usually 45,000 words or more.

novella—A fictional work, usually between 7,500 and 40,000 words.

outline—A list of bullet points or short sentences that describe the action or major scenes in a story, chapter by chapter.

payment on acceptance—A business agreement in which the author receives payment only after the editor accepts a finished piece of writing.

payment on publication—A business agreement in which the author receives payment only when a piece is published.

payment on spec—The submission of a piece of writing with no obligation or guarantee that it will be published.

pantster—A writer who just sits down and writes with little preparation. Comes from the expression, "by the seat of the pants."

plotter—A writer who plans ahead. One who organizes ideas and story elements before beginning to write.

POD—Print-On-Demand, a process that allows you to order a small number of printed books and pay for them when they're printed.

POV—Point of view.

premise—A set of circumstances the reader must accept as the basis of the story. Unless the story is fantasy, the premise should be believable.

protagonist—Main character, hero or heroine.

purple prose—Writing that is so flowery and extravagant that it stands out in sharp contrast to the other writing around it.

query letter—Also known as a pitch letter. A brief (usually one page) letter that outlines your story idea. It explains what your proposed article or book is about and why it would appeal to readers.

RITA—Awards for contest winners, given by RWA.

RWA—Romance Writers of America.

slush, slush pile—Publisher's accumulation of unsolicited (and often unread) manuscripts.

synopsis—A short description of a story or book, usually written so as to capture the reader's interest without giving away the plot or ending.

tag—A linking verb that identifies the speaker in dialogue and, often, how the dialogue was delivered. Common tags are "he said," and "she said." Other verbs can be used, for example, *shouted, asked, replied*, and so on. Also called **tag line** or **dialogue tag**.

An **action tag** indirectly implies the speaker and manner in dialogue. For example: *She shot him a withering look. "How dare you!"*

An **emotional tag** shows, without telling, some kind of feeling in the dialogue. For example, *She clutched the picture, unaware she was crumpling it ... "So it's true?"*

troll—A troublesome person on the Internet who promotes discord and harsh criticism, stirring up trouble and controversy, apparently for attention.

trope—A common writing device or motif, often overused until it becomes a cliché.

About Jane Porter

Bestselling author Jane Porter has been a finalist for the prestigious RITA award four times and has over 12 million copies in print. Jane's novel, Flirting With Forty, picked by Redbook as its Red Hot Summer Read, went back for seven printings in six weeks before being made into a Lifetime movie starring Heather Locklear. A mother of three sons, Jane holds an MA in Writing from the University of San Francisco and makes her home in sunny San Clemente, CA with her surfer husband.

Jane is the founder of The Tule Publishing Group, LLC.

Visit Jane at www.JanePorter.com.

Other Contributors

Kim Boykin

Kim Boykin is a women's fiction author with a sassy
Southern streak. She is the author of The Wisdom of Hair,
Steal Me, Cowboy, and Palmetto Moon (Summer 2014.)
While her heart is always in South Carolina, she lives in
Charlotte, North Carolina, with her husband, three dogs,
and 126 rose bushes.

Visit Kim at www.KimBoykin.com.

CJ Carmichael

Credit: jodiophotography.com

CJ has published over 35 novels and has twice been nominated for a RITA award. She likes to write stories about romance, family and intrigue, usually in small town or rural settings. When it's time to take a break from the computer, she heads to the Rocky Mountains near her home in Calgary where she lives with her partner Michael and their cat, Penny.

Visit CJ at www.CJCarmichael.com.

Megan Crane

USA Today bestselling author Megan Crane writes women's fiction, chick lit, work-for-hire YA, and a lot of Harlequin Presents as Caitlin Crews. She also teaches creative writing classes both online at mediabistro.com and at UCLA Extension's prestigious Writers' Program, where she finally uses the MA and PhD in English Literature she received from the University of York in York, England. She currently lives in California, with her animator/comic-book artist husband and their menagerie of ridiculous animals.

Visit Megan at www.MeganCrane.com.

Lilian Darcy

Lilian Darcy was born on Valentine's Day. This auspicious date, as well as a love of reading, set her destiny as a writer of romance and women's fiction from an early age. She has also written extensively for Australian theatre and television, under another name. Her plays have been professionally performed by some of Australia's most prestigious theatre companies, and have received two award nominations for Best Play from the Australian Writers Guild, while in 1990 she was the co-recipient of an Australian Film Institute award for best TV mini-series. She has now written over eighty romances for Harlequin, as well as several mainstream novels, including *Cafe du Jour*, originally published by Mira Books Australia.

Visit Lilian at www.LilianDarcy.com.

Meghan Farrell

A native Texan, Meghan graduated from The University of Texas at Austin with a degree in Psychology. She recently packed up her bags and moved to the Golden State, where she is the Manager of Marketing and Production for Tule Publishing Group in San Clemente, California. Meghan enjoys sharing her enthusiasm for travel, a good cup of coffee, and a great book!

Visit Meghan at www.TulePublishing.com.

Anne Gracie

Anne is a former president of Romance Writers of Australia, a three time RITA finalist, has twice won the Romantic Book of the Year (Australia) and the National Reader's Choice Award (USA) and has been listed in Library Journal (USA) best books of the year. Her latest book, *The Autumn Bride*, is the first in the Chance Girls series.

Visit Anne at www.AnneGracie.com.

Katherine Garbera

USA Today bestselling author Katherine Garbera is a two-time Maggie winner who has written more than 60 books. A Florida native who grew up to travel the globe, Katherine now makes her home in the Midlands of the UK with her husband, two children and a very spoiled miniature dachshund.

Visit Katherine at www.KatherineGarbera.com.

Kelly Hunter

Accidentally educated in the sciences, Kelly Hunter didn't
think to start writing romances until she was surrounded
by the jungles of Malaysia for a year and didn't have
anything to read. Kelly now lives in Australia, surrounded
by lush farmland and family. Kelly is a USA Today
bestselling author, a three-time RITA finalist and loves
writing to the short contemporary romance form.

Visit Kelly at www.KellyHunter.net.

Rebecca Lyles

Rebecca is a business consultant, editor, and blogger. After a long career in high-tech big business, she finally gave in to her destiny. Named after Daphne du Maurier's classic, how could she *not* end up in fiction? She lives in Laguna Beach California, where she edits romances, mysteries, thrillers... and technical non-fiction as Text CPR, LLC.

Visit Rebecca at www.TextCPR.com.

Anne McAllister

Anne McAllister has written over 60 romance novels as well as novellas and a single title. She is a two-time RITA award winner and a nine-time finalist. In 2000, she was named Midwest Fiction Writers "Writer of the Year" and also received Romantic Times Career Achievement Award as "Series Author of the Year."

Anne grew up on the beaches of southern California, and spent summers in Montana and Colorado. They were formative experiences—not only in providing her settings, but in giving her heroes. Lean, dark, honorable men—often lone wolf types—who always get the job done.

Visit Anne at www.AnneMcallister.com.

Melissa McClone

Melissa McClone's degree in mechanical engineering from Stanford University led her to a job with a major airline where she traveled the globe and met her husband. But analyzing jet engine performance couldn't compete with her love of writing happily ever afters. Since then, she has published over twenty-five romance novels with Harlequin and been nominated for Romance Writers of America's RITA award. Melissa lives in the Pacific Northwest with her husband, three school-aged children, two spoiled Norwegian Elkhounds and cats who think they rule the house.

Visit Melissa at www.MelissaMcClone.com.

Trish Morey

Trish Morey writes romance novels for Harlequin Mills & Boon. She grew up reading romance novels and dreamed of writing her own one day. Her novels have won many awards and Morey is the Published Author Liaison for Romance Writers of Australia. Morey lives with her husband and their daughters in South Australia.

Visit Trish at www.TrishMorey.com.

Tessa Shapcott

Tessa is a freelance editor and editorial consultant. She works with a variety of clients, from well-known published writers to mainstream and online digital publishers and aspiring writers. She is also a published romance genre writer and an Associate Vice President of the Romantic Novelists' Association. Tessa has over thirty years' experience working in the book publishing industry and is a RITA award-winning editor.

Visit Tessa at www.TessaShapcott.com.

Nancy Robards Thompson

Award winning author Nancy Robards Thompson lives in Florida, but her imagination transports her all over the world. She earned a degree in journalism only to realize reporting "just the facts" bored her silly. Nancy has found Nirvana doing what she loves most – writing contemporary and historical women's fiction. This two-time nominee for the Romance Writers of America's Golden Heart struck gold in July 2002 when she won the award. Since then, she's gone on to publish 22 books, which critics have deemed, "...funny, smart and observant."

Visit Nancy at www.NancyRobardsThompson.com.

For all the latest news and fun from
The Tule Publishing Group, visit our website:
www.TulePublishing.com

~ Lucy ~
Wardrobe - person - geeky -
- secretly married -